D0357046

VATICAN II IN PLAIN ENGLISH

The
Council

VATICAN II IN PLAIN ENGLISH

The
Council

by Bill Huebsch

ave maria press A̲m̲P̲ Notre Dame, IN

NIHIL OBSTAT
Rev. Msgr. Glenn D. Gardner, J.C.D.
Censor Librorum

IMPRIMATUR
† Most Rev. Charles V. Grahmann
Bishop of Dallas

November 21, 1996

The Nihil Obstat and Imprimatur are official declarations that the material reviewed is free of doctrinal or moral error. No implication is contained therein that those granting the Nihil Obstat and Imprimatur agree with the contents, opinions, or statements expressed.

ACKNOWLEDGMENT
The detail of the cover photo collage depicting the bishops at the council is reprinted with permission from Chr. Belser Verlag AG für Verlagsgeschäfte & Co. KG. From Wolleh, Das Konzil, Stuttgart 1965.

Scripture quotations are adapted from the *New Revised Standard Version* of the Bible, copyright 1989 by the Division of Christian Education of the National Council of the Churches of Christ in the USA. Used by permission. All rights reserved.

www.avemariapress.com

Book One   ISBN-10 1-59471-105-4   ISBN-13 978-1-59471-105-3
Book Two   ISBN-10 1-59471-106-2   ISBN-13 978-1-59471-106-0
Book Three ISBN-10 1-59471-107-0   ISBN-13 978-1-59471-107-7
Set   ISBN-10 1-59471-108-9   ISBN-13 978-1-59471-108-4

Printed in the United States of America

CONTENTS

Chapter Four
The Council Itself

Appendix One
A Brief Summary of the Documents of Vatican II

*This book is dedicated
to the memory of
Pope John XXIII*

Prologue

❋

*I*t's been more than thirty-five years since Pope John XXIII announced that there would be a worldwide council of the Church. And it's been more than thirty years since the last session of that council ended under the leadership of Pope Paul VI. So, unless you're a real student of history, you might be wondering why you should read a series of books about Vatican II. Maybe you weren't even born when this council did its work. Maybe you think you learned all there is to know at parish education forums immediately after the council. Maybe you think it's high time for Vatican III to get under way! Or maybe you don't even know what we're talking about when we use the term *Vatican II*.

Well, whoever you are, I've met many of you a hundred times as I've traveled the part of the world in which I've been ministering. I've met you at initiation workshops, liturgy conferences, and religious education congresses across the United States, Canada, and Europe. And together in the process, you and I have seen both an enthusiastic embrace of the spirit of Vatican II, as well as a much more resistant neglect of its teachings. We've seen a Church at home in the new world it helped found through the spirit and insight of this council, as well as a Church more frightened of the modern times. We've redefined ourselves as Church, "the people of God" as the council named us, united by a common baptism and ready for ministry. And, on the other hand, we've seen ourselves become polarized and divided over the very issues of ministry and discipline which define us most.

During the same month in which I read the manuscript for Bill Huebsch's books, four events occurred in my life that have clarified my response to the question I posed above, "Why would anyone want to read this series of books, *Vatican II in Plain English?*"

First, I recently attended an institute for the Christian initiation of children. While there, I fell into a discussion about the theology of confirmation with a young mother who is also a catechist. She was born after Vatican II had ended. As she became aware that the shifts in theory and practice that have emerged since she was a child were linked to Vatican II, she exclaimed, "What council?! No one sent *me* a memo about this!"

Second, I read an article in the daily paper which included an excerpt from Cardinal Joseph Bernardin speaking about polarization in today's Church. As he invited various parties in the Church to join a dialogue with him and each other about their various positions, he noted that there is an evident "mean-spiritedness" present which seems to him to be out of step with the Gospel.

Third, my younger sister gave me a copy of a book entitled *What God Allows: The Crisis of Faith and Conscience in One Catholic Church,* which I promptly read. This book describes her parish, as well as many of us in the Church today, many of the people I've met over the years. It provided me with a penetrating report on the inner life of this parish and indeed of the whole Church!

Finally, I read the text of Archbishop John Quinn's 1996 address at Oxford University in which he called for more dialogue in the Church. He cited numerous matters that were either issues on the agenda of Vatican II, such as the role of the Roman Curia in the governance of the Church, or matters that were a direct result of the implementation of the council's documents in today's world, such as questions surrounding ordination, celibacy, and women.

In the midst of these events, I recalled an early-morning class on the theology of grace sometime in the 1970s at the University of Leuven. I also remembered its professor, Piet Fransen. This animated teacher had traveled back and forth to the council, talking about the importance of the "synchronicity" of events and people in the development of the theology of sacraments and grace. This important theology formed the underpinnings of the council's development of both the constitution on the liturgy and the one on the Church. In the midst of his passionate musings on this particular morning, he stopped to focus his attention on his young students. There are two things you must attend to, he told us that morning, in order to do theology. First, be aware of synchronicity and second, learn to understand that your lives will be spent as bridge builders to and from this council.

"Bridge builders *to and from this council.*" His words still ring in my ears.

Taking these events and this memory as my cue, I now propose to you my answer to that earlier question on why you or anyone should read *Vatican II in Plain English.*

Vatican II is the defining event of our Church, not just for the twentieth century but for the new millennium as well. The people who make up the vast population of today's and tomorrow's Church, like the young woman I met at the initiation institute, need to "read the memos" and know the facts behind the Church's decisions of today and yesterday.

In this series, Bill Huebsch presents the facts and the history, the chief players and the major results of Vatican II in such a clear way that people who feel uninformed about the council will finish these books equipped with balanced information about it. And people who feel hesitant about its outcomes will be reassured to discover here that it was indeed the Spirit who moved among the bishops in St. Peter's where council sessions were held.

It may be true, as Cardinal Bernardin suggests, that the implementation of the council has produced a "mean-spiritedness" among groups in the Church. But often mean-spiritedness comes from fear and lack of information. It is timely, then, for all of us to pick up this treasure and peruse it, either to refresh our memories or to learn about it for the first time.

And it may be true, as the author of *What God Allows* suggests, that parish life is loaded with dilemmas as polarized people sort out how to form a single church community in that parish. But through *Vatican II in Plain English*, the reader will quickly realize that similar dilemmas were sorted out by the bishops and advisors at the council in Roman coffee bars and at papal dining tables. Such dilemmas and our struggle to balance them are not new.

And it may also be true, as Archbishop Quinn suggested in his remarks at Oxford, that more reform and more dialogue are needed today. This series helps us see such a call for continued reform as part of the "significant historic shift" in which we as Church are still involved, a shift which Vatican II itself promoted.

Maureen A. Kelly

Introduction

※

I decided to write this book in 1982. That year I was traveling extensively in the towns and villages of the Diocese of New Ulm in rural Minnesota, working with a team alongside Raymond Lucker, the bishop, to establish the RENEW program. We wanted to encourage people's faith and announce the Gospel to any who were listening for the first time. And we wanted to encourage parish leaders and baptized ministers to do the same in their work.

In the Diocese of New Ulm, the staff saw itself merely as a resource to the parishes, which is where the "real" Church lives, according to Bishop Lucker. Our task was to be, not in offices at the chancery, but in "parish meeting halls" across southwest central Minnesota.

We searched high and low for materials with which to offer people education, formation, and training. And we found many, many good things. The Catholic publishers in this country have rallied since Vatican II to provide excellent material with which to promulgate the teachings of the council itself, as well as for the study of Scripture and other essential matters.

But we did not have this book. We did not have an inexpensive, easy-to-read account of the unfolding of this historic event, the Second Vatican Council. In his opening speech, Pope John XXIII said that the council was now about to rise in the Church "like a daybreak, a forerunner of a most splendid light!" It is without doubt the most central and influential event in the Church since the sixteenth century.

But few people, including the pastoral staff, understood it deeply. Few knew its story well.

While in graduate school at the Catholic Theological Union in Chicago, I had studied under Father Ted Ross, a Jesuit church historian and expert on the council. He presented all of this material in very plain English, while still offering the key details and original sources to make it possible for his students to appreciate this council *in its most real context*, that is, in the Church that received it.

The council was a huge and dynamic event, filled with all the foibles and politics, as well as the successes and heroics one would find in any such gathering of human beings. The stories of what happened there are touching sometimes and funny other times. They tell of major turning points as the council progressed, as well as of moments when it looked very much as if we might turn back in fear. Ted Ross brought all of this to light with humor, kindness, and love for the Church.

Because of my experience with that class, I knew that I could make the documents simple for a wider audience than just that classroom at the theological union in Chicago. I knew we could "get out the word" and have it be heard everywhere, even in our parish meeting halls.

My Audience

In preparing this book now, quite a few years after I decided to write it, I have many years of those parish meeting halls behind me. That's important because it's here, among the hot dishes and pots of egg coffee, that the Church is most "at home." This is where all the efforts of this council are directed. And it's in our parish sanctuary—where we assemble to enact that most powerful and sublime human activity, the Mass—that the council spent its energy and left its heart. So as I wrote this I kept in mind all of *us:* everyday Catholics.

But I also had in mind some others, mainly Eastern Orthodox Catholics, other Christians, Jews, and Catholics exiled by their own church for various reasons. This council opened a huge door and extended a warm hand for the first time in many years. For Jews, the separation had been long and extremely painful, 2,000 years without meaningful dialogue and understanding. For Eastern Orthodox folks, we'd been separated since 1054 or longer. For Christian churches that emerged after the Reformation, it had been more than four hundred years of hatred and animosity. And for Catholics exiled by their own church, it had been generations upon generations of broken families and broken hearts.

I want you all to know this story and to appreciate the really significant historic shift in which the Roman Catholic Church is still involved.

My great hope is that, by knowing how this happened and by understanding its outcomes, we will all find the energy and will to continue reforming ourselves. We will all, I hope, desire greater unity with each other. We will all, I hope, live more fully in the Light.

Sources

To prepare this text, I have gone to the sources considered trustworthy by everyone, including the final published documents from the council, both the English translations as well as their original Latin. I have also pored over the "daybooks" of the council published in English, giving the day-to-day details. I have found and studied the reflections of the council's participants, both the bishops and the theological experts who were present.

I have also read and reread the accounts given by Xavier Rynne, still an absolutely excellent telling of the story, and Bob Kaiser's excellent coverage, which appeared first in *Time* magazine, as well as many other commentaries, news articles, and theological texts. I have also participated in the Liturgy of the Church, that place where, week after week, we experience firsthand the life we share together. And, as I said above, I have listened to question after question about the council coming from folks in the meeting halls of our parishes.

Format

I took all of that material and sought a format in which to best present a summary of the council and its documents. I decided on a fourfold approach. I chose "sense lines" to present certain kinds of material, including key speeches and statements. Sense lines allow for the juxtaposition of ideas and the isolation of key thoughts and phrases, and they make for a more poetic, almost verbal, text.

I chose "time tables" to present the actual unfolding of the council itself. This allows the reader to see the sequence of events in a summary form. I chose "lists" to give a treatment of some of the interesting details and biographical information. And I chose "common paragraphs" to give details of previous councils and historical material about the Second Vatican Council.

The Series

Finally, I decided to put this material into a small series of books. The first is the introductory material, which you can use as a discussion guide in parishes and homes or simply read to gain a deeper understanding of what happened at Vatican II.

The second and third books present the council documents themselves, but I have paraphrased these for ease in reading. Moreover, I present them entirely in sense lines, making them more accessible. In preparing those texts, I worked very closely with another theologian, Paul Thurmes, who helped make the texts as objective as possible. In these two books, Paul served as an actual coauthor on six of the documents.

In Sum

It's still much too early to adequately assess the place which this council will hold in our overall history. We are only a few decades away from its close, and we have not yet implemented all that it called for. I liken this event, though, to the apostolic period of church history when the Spirit was moving with such force to establish and renew the community of Jesus Christ as a community of love and justice, peace and openness.

Let me quote from my own text to give you a glimpse of what this might mean for the world:

> The Church longs for a fresh word today,
>> and the world longs for the Church
>> to find its voice.
> I believe that these documents,
>> when read more like Scripture than theology,
>> can be the basis for that.
> If we take them seriously
>> and read them alongside the lectionary,
>> we will need no catechisms.
> We will find in them what we seek,
>> what the world seeks,
>> that fresh voice leading us for today.
> And then, just as the Scriptures are proclaimed as
>> "The Word of the Lord,"
>> so these texts would be proclaimed as
>>> "The Word of the Church."
>>>> (chapter 4, part 1)

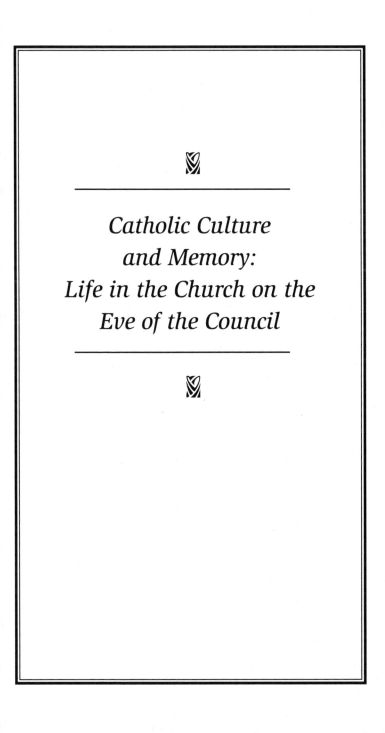

Catholic Culture
and Memory:
Life in the Church on the
Eve of the Council

Chapter One

※

*T*his is a book about Vatican II,
    the worldwide council
    of the Roman Catholic Church
    which met from 1962 through 1965 in Rome.
It's a book about its background,
    theology,
    and successful reform of the modern Church.

But it's mainly about life in the pews.

It was, after all, in the pews of the Church
    that the reforms enacted by this council
    were felt most strongly.
We all know that Vatican II restated certain doctrines
    in more modern language
    and that it modified the role of bishops
        in their relationship to the pope,
        among other things.
But its real impact,
    the place where it touched us most,
    was in the place where we could *see* the change:
        where we pray,
        at Mass.

Most Catholics
    have their primary contact with the Church
        through the Mass
        and the sacraments.

We think of ourselves as "active Catholics"
    if we attend Mass regularly,
        whether or not we're involved
        in other parish activities
        or even believe everything else
            the Church teaches.
Of course, there are also many members of the Church
    who are more active:
    sitting on parish councils,
    working in the Liturgy,
    running parish festivals,
    and providing leadership in other aspects
        of parish life.
For most, however,
    our main way of being Catholic
    is attending Mass.

But it's also a little deeper than that.

Most Catholics also believe that what happens at Mass
    cannot and does not happen anywhere else
        in the world
        or the universe.
We believe that our priests have the power
    to change the bread and wine
    into the actual Body and Blood of Christ.
This is how we identify ourselves as Catholics.
To many Roman Catholics,
    Protestant worship would always be
        slightly less powerful.
Their pastors could never enact *transubstantiation*
    during their worship.
This belief runs very deep in the Catholic mind,
    giving the Mass a natural place in Catholic thinking

as the most important human activity
    it's possible to undertake.

In the recent film *Romero*, this is made vividly clear.
It's a film about the life and death of Oscar Romero,
    the archbishop of San Salvador
    who was killed for his defense of the poor.
The filmmaker shows a moment in Romero's life
    where he was confronted by the power
    of the national army as he stood in a peasant village
        which he'd come to defend.

He was shirtless and vulnerable as he stood there.
    Their weapons were drawn and aimed at him.
    Their anger was intense.
    He appeared to be utterly powerless.
But his response was the Catholic response.
"We will now begin the Mass," he said,
    standing there in the street,
        naked,
        beaten,
        and poor.
"In the name of the Father,
    and of the Son,
    and of the Holy Spirit . . ." he began
        as he traced on his body
        the Sign of the Cross.
The camera faded back to show peasants kneeling
    in the dust of the roadway,
        signing themselves and enacting that most powerful
        of human activities:
            the Mass.

And, of course, the centrality of the Mass

was driven home even more powerfully
at the end of the film as Oscar Romero
    was murdered by an assassin,
    even as he raised the host
    during the consecration of the Mass.

After Vatican II, the Liturgy of the Word
    became a more prominent part of the Mass,
    offering Catholics more access
        to Scripture and preaching
            than before.
But in popular understanding,
    the consecration and communion
    remain the center-point of the celebration.
The old *Baltimore Catechism* taught
    that we were obliged to be present
    only for the "three principal parts of the Mass:
        the offertory,
        the consecration,
        and the priest's communion."
Some of that belief still remains.
We mess with other parts of the Mass,
    but we don't mess with the consecration
    of the bread and wine.
We replace priests when we need to for preaching,
    teaching,
    visiting the sick,
    handling the money,
    baptism,
    funerals,
    and even for the Liturgy of the Word
        in priestless parishes
        but never for this.
If there's no priest,

there's no Mass.
Period.

The Mass *is* the Church for many Catholics.
    If you took away all the other activities
        and left only the Mass,
        you'd still have the Church.
But if you took away the Mass,
    and left everything else or even increased it,
        there'd be no Church left.
It's really that central to Catholic self-identity.

Vatican II reformed the Mass,
    pulling it out of its sixteenth-century rubrics
    to reroot it in the Church's longer,
        more authentic tradition.
When it did this,
    a sea change occurred
    in Catholic self-understanding.
The council unwittingly altered far more
    than the Liturgy of the Church
    when it did its work.
It also affected a huge,
    collective,
    unconscious Catholic memory:

A memory of dark, heavy church aromas
    of incense lurking about the pews
    and beeswax candles burning silently
        at the tabernacle,
        leaving ages of sulfur behind them.
Sacristies redolent with the fragrance of spilled wines
    and the aftershave lotions of the priests.
        So many priests then.

Altar servers playing with fire,
    lighting candles and charcoal,
    fumbling with the chains of the thurible,
    tripping on the hem of life.
The faithful masses kneeling in the pews:
    patient,
    silent,
    waiting.

Genuflections were serious.
Doubles during Benediction of the Blessed Sacrament.
    God was watching.
This was *His* place,
    and there was no doubt about God's gender then.
The high ceilings and unseen crosses
    at the tops of the steeples
    made God larger than life,
        than the very life created by God.
Benediction: a brief ceremony of songs,
    poems,
    and silence
        accentuated with incense,
        holy water,
        and gold monstrances.
The monstrance: the most holy object at the parish church,
    the place where the priest put the host,
    larger than the ones you received,
        white,
        crisp,
        the Body of Christ.
Round like the moon,
    rising above the kneeling congregation,
        "exposed" for all to gaze upon
        in absolute reverence.

The Body of Christ was "exposed" in benediction,
    a vaguely,
    deeply sensual act.
I think I remember being taught
    that you weren't even supposed to *move*
    while it was visible.
Catholics fell to their knees
    to adore the sacred sacrament.
The heart and soul of being Catholic
    is believing that this, indeed,
    is the true and absolute flesh and blood
        of God's own Son.
As the *Tantum Ergo* came to a close,
    a clear and palpable sense of blessing
    descended on the congregation:
        Blessed be God.
        Blessed be His Holy Name.
        Blessed be Jesus Christ,
            true God and true Man . . .
            blessings, praises.
A sweet beatitudinal sense of well-being and honor
    fell upon everyone,
    the ones, at least, who'd stayed after Mass for this
    or who'd returned on Sunday afternoon.

And, of course, the Latin.
Memorized by priest and altar server alike,
    it added a surreal dimension to all the devotions.
God, we might have believed,
    understood our prayers better
    when they were uttered in Latin.
        Introibo ad altare Dei.
        Ad deum qui laetificat
            juventutem meam.

Could that have been true?
    Did God understand Latin better?
The Latin made the Mass seem to belong
    to someone else.
It was the bishop's
    or, more likely, the pope's Mass,
    and we were guests there,
        watching them do it.
We "attended" Mass,
    more than we "celebrated" it then.

Our main activity during Mass
    was to keep busy praying something else,
        a rosary
        or the prayers in the missal
            we'd brought with us.
There were no missalettes then,
    no song books,
    nothing in the pews to help us understand.
Then came "worship aids" after the council,
    an innovation that seemed, at first,
    an intrusion into the rosary-praying habits
        of the faithful.
How could we focus on our other prayers
    when we were "following" the missalette?!

And, then, of course,
    there was the demand that we start singing!
We were accustomed to Gregorian chant
    being sung *to us* by distant choirs
        huddled in lofts at the back of the church.
Now there were blue-jean-clad guitar players
    singing from wobbly microphones
    where the communion rail used to be.

We resented this.
    We didn't want to sing.
    We wanted to be *sung to by the choir.*
        Protestants sing;
        Catholics listen.
That's how it'd been since the sixteenth century,
    so why change it now?

But a new breed of church leader,
    known as "the liturgist,"
    was insisting that we sing.
These liturgists seemed to come from nowhere.

We'd never used the word *Liturgy* to describe Mass,
    not in common circles.
    We called it, simply, "the Mass."
They called it "the Liturgy," these new parish employees,
    which was as foreign at first as the Latin had been.
At the Liturgy, we were told plainly one Sunday,
    everyone participates, not just the priest.

Everyone understood this meant more than *watching.*

Under the old system,
    you didn't have to do much.
    You could just sit there.
And it wasn't unpleasant,
    although there was quite a bit of kneeling.
But otherwise the music was pretty,
    the smells sweet,
    and the sermons short.
The whole thing was over in fifty minutes.
There were even some legendary parishes
    where "low Mass" was over in twenty minutes!

I used to know a family
    that would drive a half-hour out of its way
    to go to a parish where the Liturgy
    was fifteen minutes shorter
        than at their own!

Participation came slowly in most places;
    centuries of silence at Mass didn't come to a halt
        very quickly.
In the beginning,
    we muttered the prayers at Mass
    almost in a whisper,
        embarrassed to be speaking out loud
        in a place where we'd been taught,
        under pain of mortal sin,
            to keep quiet.
There was always the young visiting priest
    who heard us mutter like that and said,
    "Oh come on now, people,
    you can do better than that.
Now let's try it again,
    'THE LORD BE WITH YOU!'" he'd shout.
This rebuke, of course,
    silenced half the congregation
    so that only forty dutiful mothers
        were now answering,
        making it all sound even more feeble.
"They want us to answer," we thought.
    "Why can't they just leave us alone
        so we can pray?"

Expecting us to answer the prayers out loud was one thing,
    though, while singing was another.
We just weren't used to it

and didn't want to do it.
We resisted.
We refused to open the missalette
to number 40, "Sons of God,"
no matter what they said.
Well, OK, we finally consented,
we'll open the missalette,
but we're only following along with our eye.
We aren't singing.
And, then, finally, years later,
we began to sing in that same muttery,
whispering voice with which we'd begun
to answer the prayers.
But aggressive song leaders
stood in the middle of the center aisle before Mass
rehearsing us, over and over again,
until we got it.
Until we agreed to sing.
Some people acquiesced and started singing
only as a means of getting rid
of that aggressive song leader
so we could get on with the Mass
and get home.

The song leaders weren't the only ones, though.
Where once the priest did almost everything during Mass,
except for the fumbling help of the altar servers,
now multiple people were involved.
Some were reading,
others carrying in the bread and wine.
Some were preparing the altar,
others greeting people at the door.
The Mass gradually came to look like a group activity,
like a community event.

Lay people were making announcements
    and sometimes even preaching.
Common ordinary lay people were performing jobs
    that only the priest had done for centuries.

And, then of course, there is the matter
    of *touching* the host.
Before the council,
    we were taught to go to communion
    with our hands folded and our head bowed.
We stumbled along the center aisle
    trying to recall at the last moment
    whether we'd faithfully kept to the three-hour fast
        before Mass,
        wondering whether the gum we'd chewed
            until we arrived
            may have broken that fast somehow
            as its skimpy juices made their way
                to our empty stomachs.
Wondering desperately whether there was any sin
    we'd forgotten or willfully put out of our mind
    that would force us,
        halfway down the aisle,
        to turn around red faced,
        and skulk back to our place in the pew,
            marked as the dirty sinner we were.
If we made it to the front of the church,
    we waited our turn and then knelt humbly,
    half expecting the priest to refuse to give it to us,
        and placed our hands
        beneath the white communion rail cloth,
        preventing even a tiny speck of host
            from possibly touching us.
We closed our eyes and tipped back our heads,

as the nuns had taught us to
when we were in grade school.

The priest came floating by
in his immense, fiddlebacked chasuble,
followed promptly by the altar server
with the golden plate
to catch any fragment that might escape
or to be there in case the trembling hand
of the priest fumbled the host.
Corpus Domini nostri Jesu Christi, he said.
Amen. Back to our pew.

There was a penance assigned
when you went to confession,
a small sampler of prayers to pray
before your sins were actually, totally off the slate.
That wasn't true with communion, but it felt the same.
You returned to your pew to pray.
Closing your eyes to reduce distraction
from the rest of the People of God,
you crept into silent prayer.

Then one Sunday we were surprised
with the announcement from the pulpit
that we were to take the host in our hand
and put it into our own mouth.
No more kneeling with our eyes closed,
breathless while we waited for the host
on our tongue.
It's perfectly understandable to me,
after all the practice in not doing so,
that some people felt reluctant about this.
What if a speck of that host remained on our hand

and somehow dropped off
when we weren't watching
and someone else came along and stepped on it?
Isn't every speck part of the Body of Christ?
Weren't we taught that in grade school?

This new practice felt confusing,
and some people thought that now even the bishops
must be losing their ecclesiastical minds.

It goes without saying
that we would never, ever,
have dreamed of actually drinking the wine
from the chalice.
Not even altar servers could touch a chalice.
But sure enough, pretty soon that happened too.

Not to even mention liturgical dance!
Skinny young men and women,
dressed in skimpy, wispy clothing,
not the kind of clothing we wear to church,
dancing down the center aisle
to music we didn't usually hear at Mass.
This went on only during special occasions, it's true,
but nonetheless, it was scandalous.
The only other example of this we could remember
was Herodias' daughter dancing before Herod
and his lascivious friends.
We half expected the pastor who endured this dancing
to call for someone's head on a platter himself!

And speaking of center aisles,
all of these other changes, of course,
also led to changes in where we put our furniture.

For many people, there was a great sense of loss
    in this department.
Attending Mass and contributing money were, after all,
    the measures of being a good Catholic.
And the money we gave was spent for buildings,
    by and large: bricks and mortar.
We were very rarely asked to give
    to finance dancers for Liturgy
    or for the training of small group leaders
        for renewal programs
        or any of that sort of thing.
We built buildings with our money.
The buildings were ours;
    pastors would come and go,
    traveling missionaries would come through town,
        leaning out of pulpits,
        spinning stories about the horrors of life
            on the other side of the world,
            but the building was our foundation.
Mainly, though, it was *ours*.
    It belonged to us.
    We built it.
    So don't change it.

The Church *was* its building, in many ways.
The church was concrete,
    physical,
    strong,
    a symbol of unchangeability.
        It was a fortress.
        It never changed.
            Period.
            Until now.
People showed up at their parish churches one Sunday

in the mid-1960s and found that during the week,
someone had come there with large, loud tools
and desecrated them by tearing the altar
from its place and turning it around.
They'd cut the communion rail from its hinges,
torn out the pulpit,
opened the doors,
and turned up the lights.
Minor range wars broke out in some parishes
as the faithful contributors to these buildings
tried to stop this rearrangement of the furniture
from happening.
"Don't touch my communion rail!" became the battle cry.

In one famous case a pastor feared for his safety
and escaped over the back fence of the rectory
as a truckload of angry parishioners
arrived to confront him.
The local people had formed
a "church furniture protective vigilante committee"
which tipped off a local TV camera crew,
who anticipated his escape, however,
and captured it on film for the evening news.
All he'd done was to remove the *doors*
of the communion rail
and their accompanying angels.
He felt it inappropriate to have angels
guarding the sanctuary and keeping people out.
His parishioners felt it inappropriate
to change anything whatsoever
in their parish shrine.
The doors and the angels were returned
to their original place.

And who could forget the "banner period"
    of American Catholic Church history?
This was a period of several years
    immediately following the council
    during which burlap and felt banners
        became "church art."
A whole generation of kids made banners every week
    rather than having religious education.
They learned more about glue and burlap
    than they did faith and spirituality.
It was part of the experimental search for something new
    to replace the four-hundred-year-old customs
    that had governed the Mass.
It was part of opening the windows and doors of the Church
    to let in a fresh breeze.

But, of course, the Mass wasn't all that changed.
Another major part of Catholic identity
    was our devotional life.
In "the old days" you could spot a Catholic car
    from fifty feet because there was a statue of a saint,
    normally St. Christopher,
        on the dashboard.
Devotion to the saints
    and devotions in general
    were what we did because we didn't understand
        and, therefore, couldn't really pray
            the Mass.
We used the saints to find lost things (St. Anthony),
    to bless farm fields (St. Isidore),
    and to protect us from harm (all the rest).
We wore medals around our necks,
    expecting the saint honored thereon to guard us

and asking anyone who found us dead
    to call a priest,
    a sort of Catholic dog tag.

I knew a woman once
    who believed firmly in spontaneous combustion,
    not of her or of anyone she knew,
        but of her house.
She was convinced that at any time
    her attic might burst into flames!
        (Her friends weren't sure whether
        her attic was completely lit!)
Anyway, because of this fear,
    she developed a staunch devotion
    to St. Florian, patron against home fires,
    and she gradually filled her attic
        with St. Florian medals and holy cards.
She would occasionally go up there,
    sprinkle the place with holy water,
    and read a prayer to St. Florian
        who, apparently, helped her
        since the attic survived.
This same woman, however,
    to hedge her bets,
    also kept stout ropes beneath the beds
    of her children who slept on the second floor.
She periodically ran drills with them
    during which they would tie the rope
        to a bedpost
        and shinny down to the ground
           and, presumably, to safety.
She considered the survival of her home and family
    a miracle which she attributed to St. Florian.
Mary, of course, was more.

She wasn't "just another saint."
She was the saint of the saints, the leader.
She offered Catholics a sort of female version of the deity,
    a place near God where power and glory
        were apportioned almost equally.
After all, what decent fellow
    would not want his own mother
    to have as much glory as himself?
There's really no basis for comparison
    among the holy men and women of the Church:
        Mary was The Greatest,
           The Queen.
"Holy Mary," we prayed. "Mother of God,
    pray for us sinners (she wasn't one herself, after all)
    now and at the hour of our death."

We knew she would if we asked sweetly.

What a blessing to have Mary praying for you.
Devotion to Mary, alone among devotions,
    sometimes even rivaled the Mass for its place
    in our Catholic lives.
        It was, after all,
        something we could do without a priest.
When someone died,
    the first thing a family did was to pray a rosary.
When bad weather blew in from the west,
    we headed to the basement,
    rosary cases and blankets in hand,
    to sit among the vegetables in the root cellar
        and pray to Mary for protection.
The score was pretty good:
    Mary was batting a thousand in our house.
She wasn't our only source of blessing, of course.

There was also a jar of holy water standing on
    the banister in most Catholic houses
    with which we blessed ourselves and our homes.
Every night after our bedtime prayers,
    Mom came through the house
    with the holy water jar, blessing each child
        and, finally, herself and Dad.
What a lovely gesture,
    what a loving, gentle way to enter sleep.
Each year we waited in the car after the Easter Vigil,
    the memories of those solemn ceremonies still fresh
    while the Easter bunny was on his way,
        as Mom obtained a new supply
            from the parish crock.
The parish moms seemed to like this moment in the year,
    standing among the lilies with each other,
    dressed in pink and yellow spring dresses,
    putting all their hopes for the blessing
        of their families
        into mayonnaise jars.

There were palm branches tucked each year
    behind the picture of the Last Supper
    above the buffet in the dining room.
Each year we likewise surrendered them to the priests,
    who burned them to produce the ashes
    with which we'd be signed as Lent began.

Lent.

The very word made us think about Catholic identity.
There was a custom in our public elementary school
    where each kid, on his or her birthday,
    brought a treat for everyone else.

I called home from school in third grade one day
    to ask Mom for permission to eat birthday cake
    that some Protestant kid's parents had sent
        to our classroom during Lent.
        Of all things!
        Don't they know any better?
She granted it, but I think she felt guilty about doing so.

Catholic boys, the preseminarian ones,
    kept extensive holy card collections
    like others did baseball cards,
        except our cards were blessed,
        powerful in some important, invisible way.
They had pictures of the saints on them,
    but they also had "ejaculations."
Holy card ejaculations were brief prayers one memorized
    and, periodically, spontaneously uttered!
        "All for the honor and glory of God
        and for the poor souls in purgatory!"
I later discovered the other form of ejaculation, of course,
    and I think I went into counseling
    when I realized the connection.
I still shake my head a little when I think about it.

These holy cards were icons
    of our Catholic devotional identity.
They carried an energy all their own,
    and those prayers printed on them
    were believed to merit indulgences for the user.
Catholics could build up an "account"
    of these indulgences
    counted as "days off in purgatory,"
        five hundred days for this,
        1,000 days for that.

It was all rather like a frequent flier club for Catholics
    who were willing to sacrifice themselves for God.
There were Catholic holy cards and Catholic indulgences.
    No one else had them.
As a kid, I kept a ledger book,
    recording the number of days I had earned
    and, I'm sorry to say,
    periodically drawing a thick black line
        across the page
        to start over after a mortal sin.

But collecting indulgences that way ended
    at Vatican II.
When the Mass became prayable,
    the saintly devotions became superfluous.
Grace, once dispensed in quantities of spiritual works,
    now seemed universally available.
And, in fact, the Second Vatican Council,
    going on behind our backs
        while we were still in the pews and confessionals,
            was declaring just that.
Grace is not dispensed by the Church.
It's the free gift of a loving and self-giving God,
    ours by virtue of being human.
And, furthermore,
    not particularly a Catholic item.

It would be inaccurate to paint too romantic a view
    of life in this Church
    during this period before the council.
There were also terribly fierce, inflexible rules
    which, when enforced, caused great harm.
Families expelled their children for marrying improperly,
    for divorcing,

and for failing to follow the rules exactly.
"Fallen away" Catholics were treated harshly
and excluded from Catholic circles
where they were left to roam among Protestants.
And Protestants were considered apostates and heretics,
people who had left the one true Church
and who now would not see heaven.
The unbaptized of the world,
including all the Jews, Buddhists, and others,
were simply targets for conversion to Catholicism.
Their failure to convert sentenced them to limbo at best
and to hell at worst.
There was a special disregard for the Jews,
who were considered guilty collectively
of the death of Jesus.
In general, Catholics were taught to avoid contact
with Protestants and Jews,
out of the fear that association with them
might taint the Catholic somehow.
Homosexuals were among the lowest class of persons
and guilty of unspeakable sins and vices
which could not be forgiven easily.
How they loved one another
and expressed that love through the gift of sexuality
was never a serious consideration for the Church.
It focused instead on its ruling
that such persons were simply
disordered human beings.
Unmarried pregnant women were given very little slack
and often trucked off to special "homes" for them.

Priests were often much more pastoral
than the law permitted,
but they had to be that way in secret.

From time to time the reputation of a compassionate priest
would spread in a region,
and people would go to him for confession,
knowing they would not be dealt with harshly.
And some priests, of course,
seemed to relish enforcing the law,
the letter of the law,
and condemning all who disobeyed.
Theologians who asked questions about these things
or developed creative thinking
or "out of the box" theology
were fired without explanation!
Their books were banned,
and their reputations ruined.
It was common for clergy to report on each other
for relatively minor departures from the norm,
especially when the rule breaker
was "only" an assistant pastor.

In general during this period,
the Church resisted human nature
because human nature was seen an ungodly.
Many people who today dream about church life
in the "good old days"
have forgotten about all of this pain,
all of the needlessly ruptured families,
all of the less-than-glorious guilt,
and all of the people who came for bread
but were handed only a stone.

Since the council much of this has changed
and the pastoral presence of the Church
is now more prominent.
But we still hand some of these people a stone

in our official teachings,
and there is still more work for us to do.

It was also true on the eve of the council
that Catholics were expected to live
according to a firm and unyielding
personal discipline.
Good Catholics, for example,
had refrained from eating meat on Fridays
for as long as anyone living could remember.
"Abstinence," it was called.
It was a key part of the discipline required
of faithful Catholics.
But it wasn't anything extra we did;
there weren't any special graces involved,
no indulgences.
Abstaining was just part of it
and something which set us apart
from our meat-eating, heathen Protestant neighbors.
Everyone knew it was the rule:
fish on Friday.

Fasting joined with abstinence
to round out the Catholic diet.
Before communion, we fasted to prepare ourselves
to receive the Body of Christ.
It was apparently important to do such a thing
on an empty stomach.
During Lent, the fasting rules required
that we measure our food by the ounce
to be sure we didn't eat any more
for breakfast and lunch combined
than we did for supper.
We fasted in silence,

suffering the hunger so that we could become aware
of the hunger in our hearts
    to be closer to God.

Then at the council
    or at some vague point in the early 1960s,
        this, too, began to change.
Meat was permitted again on Friday,
    fasting seemed to decline,
    and certain feast days were apparently dropped
        from the calendar altogether.
One of these was St. Christopher,
    leaving traveling Catholics high and dry
    with no patron saint and little round blemishes
        on their dashboards
        where their statue of him had been.
We felt foolish, then,
    having an icon to some saint on such public display
    when apparently not even
        the pope
        believed in such things anymore.
The "loss" of these saints
    and our dwindling devotional life
    precipitated a major change in Catholic identity.
Without public abstinence laws,
    medals around our necks,
    or dashboard reminders of our faith,
    how would anyone know we were Catholics?

If our church buildings didn't "look Catholic" anymore,
    with what would we identify?
It seemed to many Catholics
    that the Church for which they'd sacrificed
        was gone.

The Church they'd long defended against Protestantism
    had acquiesced,
    had become Protestant.
Catholic worship seemed to resemble Protestant worship,
    and Catholic teachers occasionally said
      that much of what Luther had originally wanted
        for the Church in the sixteenth century
        was probably what we needed now.
Catholics were, for God's sake,
    even being urged to read the Bible!
      Catholics reading the Bible.
      What a Protestant thought.

The shift in focus that occurred at Vatican II
    was received in a wide variety of ways
    by Catholics in the pews.
For some, the losses felt enormous,
    like losing the wind in one's sails.
For others, not enough has yet shifted and changed,
    not enough reform has been enacted.
But for all Catholics,
    and for Protestants, Jews,
    and all others of good will,
      one thing is clear:
      Vatican II did indeed occur
      and life in the Church or among the churches
        will never be the same.

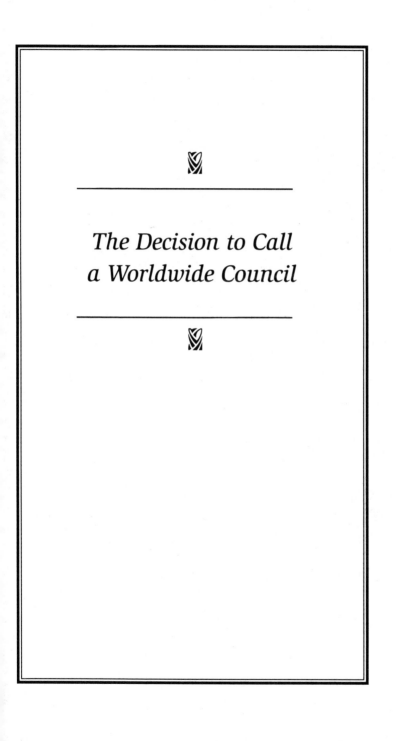

The Decision to Call a Worldwide Council

Chapter Two

⌗

PART ONE: PREPARATIONS FOR THE COUNCIL AND ITS RULES

Step One
THE ANNOUNCEMENT OF VATICAN II

*W*hy, after four hundred years of living out the decrees and rubrics of the Council of Trent, did Vatican II occur? How did the modern Church succeed in initiating such sweeping reforms? Why now? Why these particular reforms? How did all this start?

On one hand, the answer is plain: nothing less than the entire history of the Church set the stage on which this council unfolded. All of the previous twenty worldwide councils. All of the other regional and local councils and synods over the centuries. All of the theologians, reformers, popes, and leaders throughout the ages. All of the saints. All of the scandals and corruption. All faithful people, hungering for the deposit of Christian faith. All of it, the people and events of the Church's history, formed the backdrop of this council. Nothing less.

History is like that. It unfolds at its own speed like a great, centuries-long conversation, offering people in every age the opportunity to make their comments for their own day. Lucky the ones who speak up when their turn arrives, for they become the force that molds the world.

On the other hand, the answer might also have been simply that some minor event within the Vatican itself moved Pope John XXIII to decide for reform. Perhaps some petty rule was broken which resulted in a quarrel among the members of the Curia. Or perhaps some rubric was not followed, causing a scrupulous rubricist to ask the pope's forgiveness. Pope John may have said to himself, at any such moment, that *some*thing had to be done about such pettiness, *some*one had to clean out the closets of a Vatican too long without reform.

Nonetheless, the extraordinary announcement that a worldwide council of the Roman Catholic Church would be held was a surprise to everyone, including, it seems, Pope John himself. But the rise of the idea in Pope John's own mind is not complicated. He was simply struck by a strong intuition that the time for such a council was now. He became convinced in a moment of certainty that the Holy Spirit was about to hover over the Church, stirring it up, rising like daybreak, forerunning a most splendid light.

He himself told this story in his opening speech at the council. Speaking of the origin of the idea itself, he said he wished to record for history his own personal account "of the first sudden bringing up in our heart and lips of the simple words, ecumenical council. . . . It was completely unexpected," he said, "like a flash of heavenly light, shedding sweetness in eyes and hearts. And at the same time it gave rise to a great fervor throughout the world in expectation of the holding of the council."

His decision to go forward with this impulse, interestingly, did not result from a "Vatican self-study" performed by consultants and processed through endless committees, lugging ring-bound photocopies of plans, budgets, and opinion polls around the Vatican.

Rather, it resulted from his own attention to that "flash of heavenly light" which arose in his soul and breast. It resulted from his trust of that urging of the Spirit which occurred in his own heart. And he did not hesitate. He had been pope only a couple of months when this happened, scarcely time to find one's way through the labyrinthine corridors of the Vatican.

Then, speaking to seventeen cardinals at the Basilica of St. Paul-Outside-the-Walls in Rome on the feast of St. Paul, January 25, 1959, he announced his intention to hold Vatican II.

He announced, in fact, that he intended to take three extraordinary actions. He had observed, he said, the need to provide an updating of church practice and language to more adequately address the modern world. He announced, therefore, his intention (1) to hold a synod for the Diocese of Rome, of which the pope is the local bishop, (2) to hold an ecumenical council of the Church, and (3) to update the code of canon law.

(The term *ecumenical council* as it is used in reference to Vatican II does not mean that it was an "interfaith council." The term *ecumenical* used in this context simply means "worldwide." When used in most other contexts in today's Church, it means interfaith, especially between Protestants and Catholics, Anglicans and Catholics, or Jews and Catholics.)

Step Two
THE SYNOD IN THE DIOCESE OF ROME

In a sense, the second step in preparing for Vatican II was a synod in the Diocese of Rome, which was held on January 24–31, 1960. Called by the pope, this synod was intended to renew the faith of the people of Rome.

(A synod is an official meeting of the Church at pretty much any level: international, national, regional, or diocesan.

Synods usually have quite specific, limited goals and produce statements and pastoral letters aimed at guiding the Church in its everyday life.)

In order to keep this synod focused on his own desired outcomes, Pope John decided to do the speaking at the Roman synod himself. In the end, he gave several talks which treated a rather wide range of faith issues, including:

Belief in God as a Trinity of love.

Redemption from sin by the earthly sufferings and death of Jesus Christ.

The Resurrection and the hope of seeing God face to face.

The pitfalls and dangers of modern life that may lead to damnation.

For the fourth issue, Pope John insisted on the *via positiva:* Modern women and men, by putting their shoulder to the wheel of life, he argued, can achieve decency, stability, security, and a touch of holiness, no matter what the living conditions in which they find themselves.

Article 35 of the synodal statutes also provides for a more compassionate treatment of priests who have left the Church or the priesthood than was prevalent in the recent past.

Many of the notions he articulated at this synod were later reflected in the opening sections of the constitution on the Church, one of the key documents eventually emerging from Vatican II.

Step Three
CLOSE VATICAN I

Once the Roman synod was completed and its statutes promulgated, preparation of the upcoming council could get under way. The first step, a technical one, was to declare Vatican I officially closed. It had been adjourned because of the Franco-Prussian War in 1870 and the siege of Rome by Italian nationalists, but it had never been officially closed.

Step Four
PREPREPARATORY PERIOD:
WORLDWIDE CONSULTATION
ON THE AGENDA FOR VATICAN II

That done, Pope John set about preparing for Vatican II. Throughout the preparatory period, he faced stiff opposition from members of his own Curia and others who feared doom for the Church if the event were actually to occur. These church insiders, about whom he spoke in his opening speech, had come to believe that only they were able to guide and direct the Church. They feared that bringing 2,500 bishops and cardinals to Rome from all over the world, many of them already asking challenging questions, would lead only to disaster. But Pope John's resolve to proceed overrode all their concerns. It was said that each time a Vatican official approached Pope John with a suggestion for postponement of Vatican II, he advanced the target date by one month!

If this is true, it was propitious because his original plan had been to convene the council in the fall of 1963. It actually began on October 11, 1962, preceding his death by only eight months.

The formal preparation for Vatican II began with a worldwide consultation with some 2,500 residential bishops, heads of male religious orders, and faculties of Catholic universities. Just as before Vatican I, there was a desire to know what the leaders of the Church around the world believed the most pressing issues of faith to be. The consultation got under way through an invitation sent on June 18, 1959, by Cardinal Tardini, Pope John's secretary of state. The invitation asked the bishops of the world to express their desires for the council.

More than 2,000 bishops responded. Their letters were photocopied and filed. The photocopies were then cut into pieces so their various concerns could be grouped by category and subject. All of this took place on the third floor of one of the newer office buildings near the entrance to St. Peter's Square. The work was headed by Archbishop Pericle Felici, who was considered tough but conservative and who had been chosen to serve as secretary of the preparatory phase. (Archbishop Felici was later named secretary general of the council itself and proved to be an excellent one because he was a skilled Latinist and quick-witted presider. Although he favored the cause of the conservatives, he kept the meetings in order by frequent admonitions and humorous interjections which allowed for a free conciliar debate.)

The work was detailed and painstaking. Most of the responses were submitted in Latin and the effort to study them, determine their subject area, and file them appropriately was done by only five priests, working with Archbishop Felici. Once work on the bishops' responses was completed, the group set upon the responses received from the theological universities of the world, along with those received from the various offices of the Curia itself.

All of this material was eventually collated by nation and printed in book form. The books were then passed along to a group of preparatory commissions which were instituted by Pope John at a solemn Vespers on Pentecost Sunday, June 5, 1960.

Step Five
PREPARATORY PERIOD:
COMMISSIONS ARE FORMED TO DRAFT
SCHEMATA FOR THE COUNCIL

Pope John issued a *motu proprio* on June 5, 1960, announcing that the prepreparatory work was completed and that "the time had come to proceed, with God's help, to the setting up of the commissions which would devote themselves to the study of the matters that would be discussed at the council." These commissions, he went on to say, would be composed of cardinals, bishops, and other church workers noted for their virtue and learning, from both the diocesan and religious clergy, chosen from different parts of the world, so that, in this respect also, the catholicity of the Church might be displayed.

(A *motu proprio* is a papal statement which is prepared and signed by the pope himself and which states his personal wishes about a matter. In the hierarchy of papal pronouncements, *motu proprios* rank quite high.)

On this occasion Pope John also outlined what he wanted the operating procedure for this council to be. It would begin, he said, with an introductory and exploratory phase which was just concluded. It would then proceed into a preparatory phase which was begun that day. The preparatory period would be under the guidance of the commissions that he was establishing, coordinated by a central commission that would prepare position papers, called schemata, for the bishops of the world to consider in the general meetings of the council itself. The final phase of council proceedings, Pope John said in this address, would be the promulgation of the outcomes.

In this same address, he drew a distinction between the running of day-to-day church matters by the Curia and the work of this council. The pope explained that "the preparation of the council would not be the task of the Roman Curia but, together with the illustrious prelates and consultors of the Roman Curia, bishops and scholars from all over the world will offer their contributions. This distinction is therefore precise: the ordinary government of the Church with which the Roman Curia is concerned is one matter, and the council another."

Behind the scenes, the officials of the Curia viewed all this rapid preparation with attitudes ranging from passive agreement and light cooperation to outright alarm. They seemed not to trust the pope, not to believe he understood the Church and the world as they did. They seemed to believe that only they could properly settle questions of the modern Church. Realizing that they were not loved throughout the world, the officials of the Curia seemed to fear that assembling all the bishops of the Church in Rome would strip them of their power.

They also feared the liturgical movement, which was strong in northern Europe, Canada, and the Midwestern United States. They were already flooded with demands for the use of the vernacular language, something Luther had wanted! They also considered the new approach to biblical study dangerous, even though it was based on Pius XII's own encyclical *Divino Afflante Spiritu*.

These fearful Vatican insiders saw the new theological movements—especially those in Germany, Austria, Holland, France and Belgium—as a threat from the North, just as their predecessors had seen the Reformation of the sixteenth century. These modern reformers seemed to want many of the same things Luther, Calvin, and Zwingli had: vernacular language in the Mass and other sacraments, biblical study by lay people, the reform of the clergy and episcopacy, and a restructuring of the Curia with a more collegial approach to authority. "Here they come again!" they must have thought. In Rome, memories are long and time passes slowly. To these members of the Curia, it must have seemed as though all these questions had just been settled recently, even though *recently* would have meant four hundred years earlier.

The pope, of course, was of a different mind completely. He wanted to bring the Church up-to-date. He did not fear the biblical scholars and theologians; he looked to them to assist in preparing for his great renewal of Church life. Reunion of the Christian churches, something feared and opposed in Vatican circles, was his life dream and his heart's fondest desire.

The insiders, however, shocked by the pope's obviously firm intentions, not to mention his resistance to their warnings, rallied to control the outcomes of the council as much as possible by gaining positions of power and influence in the preparatory commissions. They appointed trusted "safe" men from various parts of the world to the leadership positions of these commissions and pointedly omitted inviting certain theologians or bishops they considered too "dangerous." They couldn't control the Central Commission (which coordinated council activities and preparation and whose president was the pope himself) so they did the next best thing. They arranged to have the conservatives (Cardinals Ottaviani, Ruffini, Siri, Pizzardo, and Marella) lead the discussions.

Furthermore, they saw to it that published reports of the preparatory meetings reflected their aims and points of view. They took great pains to develop an interlocking system of control: bishops and monsignors, all Italian, named as members of the preparatory commissions.

What was alarming for the rest of the Church was that these men felt free to attack the Church itself, but did not allow anyone else to. An example of this was an attack on the new biblical scholarship which was going on before the council and which helped give rise to a new understanding of divine revelation. Cardinal Ruffini of Palermo, himself a specialist in biblical research, rejected the new biblical studies and believed the Bible could be read only in fundamentalist, literalist terms. He published an article on page one of *L'Osservatore Romano* in June 1961 (before the first general meeting of the council) in which he directly contradicted Pius XII's encyclical on the matter, quoting the encyclical itself and calling the pope's position "absurd."

Anyone outside the Curial circle would have been shipped off to exile for such a statement: his published works would have been recalled and he would have been forced to recant. But this Curial insider was praised by his Curial colleagues for his objections and conservatism. (Ruffini and his colleagues were no doubt acting in good faith. That is, blinded by their own position as insiders, they certainly must have believed that what they did was best for the Church.)

In contrast to these church insiders were many of the bishops of the world where the Church was already undergoing rapid and massive change. Vatican II did not precipitate the modern times and modern thinking; it only gave it focus and theological reflection.

One example of this new ecclesial thinking and behavior was Bishop Dammert Bellido of Cajamarca, Peru, who declared, "One area in which, with the best of intentions, we still provoke scandal in some and disgust in others is in the lack of simplicity in the decoration of our churches and the riches with which we surround our ceremonies. In all innocence, we stretch our resources to obtain the costliest ornaments, which are in doubtful taste to begin with, while at the same time children of God are suffering from hunger, sickness, and misery. This is a true cause for scandal in the Church today. Sumptuosity is not in accord with the poverty of our age."

In many parts of the world, bishops were giving up their palaces and living among the poor. A group of bishops in Argentina became known as the "bishops with wooden crosses and crosiers." In San Antonio, Texas, Archbishop

Lucey was a champion of social justice for the braceros, or Mexican migrant workers. Even before the council, it was clear to a world observer that it was no longer "business as usual" for the modern Church.

Many other bishops in the world were well-trained theologians, reflecting on questions of faith and morals themselves, independently of the Curia. Many of them became important players at the council itself: Frings of Cologne, Lienart of Lille, Alfrink of Holland, Meyer of Chicago (the largest diocese in the world with 2.1 million Catholics at the time). Cardinal Montini is said to have taken ninety cases of books with him to Milan when he moved there from Rome to become its new archbishop (and later Paul VI).

Also among the scholarly bishops were Wright of Pittsburgh and Hallinan of Atlanta, known for their deep understanding of the modern times and their reflection on the Church's place in them. Koenig of Vienna had written extensively on comparative religions. Bea and Suenens were theologians as well as cardinals and played major roles in leading the movement for reform at the council.

Bishops all over the world were struggling long before Vatican II to find ways to make the modern Church more compelling for the modern times. Experiments were going on in many parts of the world, from India, where Bishop Pereira had visited every village along the coast to introduce a program of modern social development, to Latin America, where bishops were taking up residence as pastors among the poor.

Meanwhile, the preparation by the commissions established by Pope John continued under the influence of all these forces, gradually coalescing in the months before the council to set the stage for the great debates that eventually occurred there.

Step Six
POPE JOHN ISSUES COUNCIL RULES
AND PROCEDURES

The rules and procedures under which the council would operate were established and published by another *motu proprio* issued on September 5, 1962, only five weeks before the council opened. In this pronouncement, the pope:

named a presiding council,

named cardinals of the Curia to head the ten council commissions responsible for the working documents,

appointed Cardinal Cicognani, the pope's secretary of state, as president of a special office that would oversee unforeseen problems at the council,

required a two-thirds majority (in addition to his own approval) to enact decrees at the council itself, and regulated the rest of the voting,

invited non-Catholic observers to attend both the solemn public sessions and also the actual working sessions in which all the bishops would take part,

required bishops to remain in Rome throughout the council sessions and to leave only if they were given explicit permission to do so,

established that the meetings of the council would be held at the Vatican in St. Peter's,

directed what the bishops, abbots, and other prelates were to wear to the various council sessions ("At the public sessions all the fathers having episcopal rank . . . will wear a white cope and miter. But at the general congregations [daily meetings] the cardinals will wear red or violet cassocks, according to the liturgical season, with rochet, short cape, and mozzetta; patriarchs will dress in violet . . . abbots . . . will wear their own choir dress"),

established norms for a profession of faith and an oath of secrecy regarding council proceedings,

prescribed that Latin would be the only language that could be used at public sessions and most other meetings: "At the meetings of the council commissions modern languages can also be used in addition to Latin, but subject to immediate translation into Latin,"

indicated how the discussion at the general sessions would proceed: introduction of the topic with a brief explanation, speeches for or against which must stick to the topic and not exceed ten minutes of length, voting on amendments, revision of the documents, resubmission of the total schema, more voting, eventual promulgation if it pleased the council fathers and the pope.

Step Seven
THE BISHOPS' ARRIVAL IN ROME
AND THE BEGINNING OF THE COUNCIL

With all this preparation completed, the day finally arrived for travel to Rome. In chanceries, monasteries, and universities all over the world, bishops, abbots, and theologians turned their attention to preparing to depart. Gradually, in the fall of 1962, they packed up their vestments, books, and council agendas and headed to the Eternal City.

The Vatican, having no major inn, could not house so many people, so the travelers took up residence in monasteries, convents, small inns, rectories, and university housing all over the city of Rome.

Many of world's bishops traveled to the council accompanied by small groups of staff members to assist them with translation and research. Some of the Germans are even said to have brought their own printing presses to Rome, apparently aware of the Italian sense of urgency when deadlines were involved. Having translators and presses handy would allow them to make the Latin documents as well as various theological position papers widely available in the city of Rome to facilitate the adoption of reforms.

Indeed, this council would undertake major questions that had lain before the Church for many, many centuries without open discussion:

> the role of bishops in their relationship to the bishop of Rome (also known as the pope),

> the place and role of lay people in the life and operations of the Church,

> the understanding and place of religious liberty in the modern Church,

> the Church's teaching on divine revelation and its source,

> the Church's attitude toward and desire for relationship with the Jews,

> the way Christian unity would be approached,

> the reform and restoration of the Liturgy, the catechumenate, the diaconate, and the place of

the laity in them,

and most remarkably and without precedence, the
place and relationship of the Church to the whole
modern world, with all its new challenges and
needs, including its place in the lives of all people:
Catholics, other Christians, non-Christians,
nonbelievers, and all people of good will.

The Second Vatican Council was now set to begin.

PART TWO: POPE JOHN XXIII ANNOUNCES THE SECOND VATICAN COUNCIL

Made at the Basilica of St. Paul-Outside-the-Walls
January 25, 1959

Paraphrase Text

I am prompted
    to open my mind and heart to you,
    because of this feast
    of the Conversion of St. Paul.
I want to tell you frankly
    about several points
    of planned pastoral activity
    which have emerged in my thoughts
    because of my brief three months here
    within these church circles in Rome.
In doing so,
    I am thinking of the care of the souls of the faithful
        in these modern times.
I know that everyone is watching me
    as the new pope,

wondering what kind of time
this will be
for the Church.
I am gradually settling into my new role
and beginning to see how it will fit
into the overall history of the Church.
As you know, I have a double responsibility
as both bishop of the Diocese of Rome
and shepherd of the universal Church.
I am paying attention to both of these,
as I should.
First, let me reflect on the city of Rome.
It is much changed since my own youth
and is now a bustling city
with rapid growth,
especially in the suburbs,
struggling at times
to be a unified city
and community.
I have been briefed on the spiritual condition
of the people in Rome
and I am pleased with the wonderful efforts
of the cardinal vicar,
who handles the day-to-day activities
of this local diocese.
He and his staff have been vigilant and zealous
in providing for the local needs.
But, on the other hand,
I remember the story in the Gospels
when the great crowds called on Jesus
to help them find nourishment
and grace.
It touches my heart as I think of it:

a few loaves, a few fish,
"What are these among so many?"
This says it all:
    an increase in energies
    and a more coordinated effort
        will, with God's help,
            produce great fruits!
I fervently desire this more fruitful
    and deeply spiritual life for the Church.
It is a happy thing to see the grace of Christ
    multiplied throughout the world
    and providing guidance and blessing
        for everyone.
But I am saddened when people forget
    the place of God in their lives
    and pursue earthly goods,
        as though they were an end in themselves.
I think, in fact, that this blind pursuit
    of the things of this world
    emerges from the power of darkness,
        not from the light of the Gospels,
        and it is enabled by modern technology.
All of this weakens the energy of the spirit
    and generally leads to divisions,
        spiritual decline,
        and moral failure.
As a priest, and now as the shepherd of the Church,
    I am troubled and aroused
    by this tendency in modern life,
        and this makes me determined
        to recall certain ancient practices
        of the Church
            in order to stem the tide
            of this decline.

Throughout the history of the Church,
 such renewal has always yielded wonderful results.
It produces greater clarity of thought,
 solidarity of religious unity,
 and abundant spiritual riches in people's lives.
So now, trembling a bit with emotion,
 I announce to you my intention
 to hold a twofold event:
  a diocesan-wide meeting for this city
  and an ecumenical council
   for the universal Church.
And this will also lead to a bringing up-to-date
 of the code of canon law,
 which will accompany and crown
  these other two events.
For the moment, my announcement to you
 is sufficiently made,
 and I will also announce this myself
 to the rest of the cardinals of the world.
I would be happy to hear your opinion of this
 and also grateful for your suggestions
 as to how to best carry out this triple plan.
In moving forward like this,
 I am trusting in God's grace,
 as well as the protection and intercession
  of Mary and the saints.
I beg them for blessings on this work:
 a good beginning,
 a blessed continuation,
 and a happy outcome.
We think this will produce a great enlightenment
 for all Christian people
 as well as a renewed invitation
  to our separated sisters and brothers

so that all may follow us in this search
for unity and grace.
In closing, let me recite the blessing of St. Leo the Great,
which is so fitting for this moment in time:
"You are my crown and my joy
if your faith,
which from the beginning of the Gospels
is preached throughout the world,
perseveres in sweetness and holiness."
Oh! What a greeting this is,
wholly worthy of our spiritual family.
I bless you in the name of the Father
and of the Son
and of the Holy Spirit. Amen.

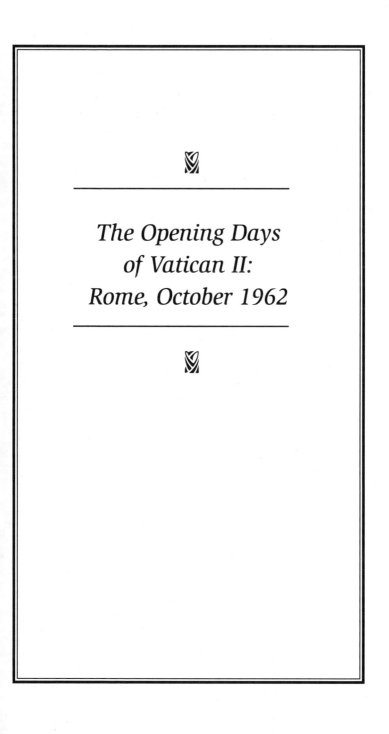

*The Opening Days
of Vatican II:
Rome, October 1962*

Chapter Three

※

PART ONE: OPERATIONS AND LOGISTICS

The Opening Procession

*E*arly on the morning of Thursday, October 11, 1962, a large crowd gathered in St. Peter's Square in Vatican City, Rome. The crowd waited to witness a historic event, so grand in scale and so unusual that few could have understood completely what they were about to see.

For it was on this day that the windows of the Church were thrown open by Pope John XXIII. They were thrown open and light burst into the chambers, long darkened by a too-rigid, too-triumphal application of the decrees of the Council of Trent.

Everyone standing there that morning must have been stirred when, at precisely 8:00 A.M., two papal guards in dress uniform slowly drew open the doors to the papal apartments on the north side of the square. These great bronze doors stand at the head of Bernini's *Scala Regia*, the staircase leading to the apartments of the pope. Behind these doors stood row upon row of bishops, patriarchs, archbishops, abbots, and scarlet-clad cardinals, all under the command of the papal master of ceremonies. They were poised to descend the stair and the whole spectacle must have resembled some medieval Byzantine ceremony.

They did march out of the Vatican palace, down into the well-guarded square, a seemingly endless number of them, more than 2,500 in all! Beneath their miters or other headdress, their faces were the colors of the world. More than 500 of them were from South America, 126 were native Asians, 118 were native Africans. (At Vatican I, only 55 of the attendees were not European, and none of them was native Asian or African.)

Slowly they moved across the square, swinging to the right as they moved out of the staircase, then right again to mount the huge, sprawling steps of the basilica.

Finally, as the cardinals moved down the stairs, across the square, and into the church, the pope appeared. He was being carried on the *sedi gestatoria,* waving warmly in response to the acclamation of the crowd. He offered them his blessing. He smiled as he was moved through them and wept quietly. What must have been his thoughts that day? What must have he borne in his heart as this event unfolded, initially against the wishes of all his Vatican advisers?

Pope John's Opening Address

The prelates celebrated the Mass of the Holy Spirit, chanting the readings in both Latin and Greek to signify the unity of East and West. Then the pope delivered his sermon, a keynote that would set the tone and agenda for the council. In clear, resonant Latin that was well heard throughout the basilica, he said he was tired of listening to the negative tones of his advisors. "Though burning with zeal," he said, "they are not endowed with very much sense of discretion or measure." These, the pope said, believe that our modern times, compared to past ages in the Church, are somehow worse, and, he said, "they behave as though they had learned nothing from history, which is nevertheless the great teacher of life."

"We feel that we must disagree with these prophets of doom, who are always forecasting disaster as though the end of the world were at hand," the pope added.

With these opening words, Pope John XXIII gave perspective to much that had gone on during the preparation period of the council. Seated there with him were the very doomsayers he was describing: Cardinal Ottaviani (seated at his immediate right hand), Cardinals Siri and Ruffini, Pericle Felici, Enrico Dante (papal master of ceremonies), and many others. These had been the obstructionists during the preparatory period, and they must have felt the heat of the pope's words as they sat there that day. As he went on to outline his intentions for the council, they must have wondered where this would lead.

The pope left no doubt about that.

"Divine Providence," the pope continued, "is leading us to a new order of human relations." How well this pope knew that. How well this comment reflected the newly emerging life of the modern Church where bishops were pastors rather than canon lawyers. It's time, the pope went on to say, for the Church "to bring herself up-to-date where required." His wishes were clear; there would be *aggiornamento* in the Church.

(*Aggiornamento* is an Italian word that has come to signify the throwing open of the Church's windows to allow reform and freshness to replace all that has grown stale. It means, more literally in Italian, to make things ready for today, today's needs, today's times, today's people.)

Pope John went on to say that he had not called the council so that a new doctrine or dogma could be defined. A council, he said, would not be necessary for that. Rather, he said, "the world expects a step forward toward doctrinal penetration and the formation of consciences," and this work would proceed by employing methods of research and literary forms of modern thought.

"The substance of the ancient doctrine" of the faith is one thing, he said, "the way in which it is expressed is another." With this he called for new ways of teaching the truths of the faith and for a contemporary language to express the truth. Such a new language, of course, would never be adequate, just as past attempts at expressing the truth had not been. But a new expression would fit these times more appropriately.

The pope explicitly declared that this council would not include the condemnation of anyone. "Nowadays the Bride of Christ prefers to make use of the medicine of mercy rather than that of severity," he explained. "She considers that she meets the needs of the present day by demonstrating the validity of her teaching rather than by condemnation."

John concluded by speaking about the unity of the human family. The key, he said, to such unity, including not only Christians but "those who follow non-Christian religions," would be love, "the fullness of charity," as he put it.

The pope's inaugural address marked the end of a period of intransigence and rigidity in the Church that began with the Council of Trent in the sixteenth century. It opened the doors of the Church to renewal and reform. It heartened the leaders of this reform while at the same time it made possible the open debates which characterized Vatican II. It prevented the council from focusing on the definition of new doctrine or condemnation of error, on which all previous councils had focused. From that point forward, the work of the council belonged to the bishops, and following this address, the pope did not enter the hall again until the end of the first session.

Council Operations and Logistics

Much of the actual preparation for the operations of the council itself was done by members of the Vatican offices which govern the worldwide Church. Taken together these offices are known as the Curia. (The term *curia* originated in the ancient Roman world. It referred to the meeting place of the senate at Rome, most likely that begun by Julius Caesar in 44 before the new era.)

These curialists, as they are known, had urged the pope to insist upon the use of Latin as the official language of the council. Latin was not the language, of course, of the Eastern rites, nor of Protestant or Jewish guests. It was not spoken on a day-to-day basis in most of the Church. But it was the traditional language of church ritual and official texts. (It's curious that a council whose stated agenda was to update the Church for the modern times would use for its discourse and official documents a language that had not been modern for many centuries. But Latin it would be.)

Certain prelates, especially seminary professors, were able to speak Latin quite well and, therefore, rose as leaders quickly. They included Siri of Genoa, Italy; Suenens of Malines, Belgium; Doepfner of Munich, Germany; and Leger of Montreal, Canada. Others had to rely on their experts, known as *periti*, for translations because no translation equipment was provided to council fathers. Most could have used such help.

It must have occurred to the council's organizers that no real debate would occur in Latin. The papers presented in the council hall were formal, though brief. But council sessions were not usually the scene of much actual interchange. Only a few prelates in the world would have been capable of a sustained spontaneous discussion in Latin. The result of this latinization of the council was, of course, that the real debates occurred elsewhere. Where?

By any measure, 2,500 cardinals, patriarchs, archbishops, and bishops, along with their staff, are a large number of guests. They could not, of course, lodge in the Vatican since only a small number of guest rooms are available there. So they lived instead in a variety of settings all around the city of Rome.

Colleges, monasteries, convents, retreat centers, and shrines hosted many visitors. With them had gathered hundreds of theologians and canon lawyers who worked as advisers to various bishops and conferences of bishops and who also needed lodging. And there was also a massive press corps present, unlike any previous council. More than 1,000 reporters and photographers were present for the opening session.

After each day's formal council session, less formal gatherings occurred in these various residences around Rome. Here the participants could sort out the day's happenings, catch up on council gossip, and consider new ideas together.

Short speeches were often given in these evening meetings and various positions and strategies were discussed, amid vociferous debate, often including the residents of those places: seminarians, religious men and women, professors, and other locals. These local discussions often ended in a paper, summarizing a position. These position papers were then translated into many of the world's major languages and shared among the other council participants. The papers sometimes had great influence on council outcomes.

Pope John also assisted the informal debate by establishing two coffee bars adjoining the council hall in the basilica. These popular coffee shops came to be known during the council as Bar-Jonah and Barabbas. In these rooms, which were each the size of a ballroom, the council fathers competed with the *periti*, the Protestant and Orthodox observers, and their opponents in the debates, for the attention of the attendants to obtain their midmorning *cappuccino*. Here as well, less formal discussion could occur and the participants could come to know one another in a context other than the formal, Latin-dominated setting of the council session.

The seating at the council sessions themselves was prearranged by the organizers based purely on seniority, that is, on the order of appointment to the hierarchy. Participants were not seated by national groups. Hence, it would have been unlikely that council participants would be seated next to people they knew.

For many, this was an unprecedented opportunity to talk with prelates from other parts of the world. In doing so, many discovered that they shared common goals for the Church and suffered from common difficulties in carrying out practices first introduced four hundred years earlier at the Council of Trent.

Microphones were distributed throughout the nave of St. Peter's Basilica to allow for an orderly debate, although longer presentations would be made from a central podium. (No previous council had the use of microphones.) Those who wished to speak, except for the cardinals, were required to make application to the general secretary of the council beforehand.

Daily meetings called general congregations ran from 9:00 A.M. until around 12:15 P.M. They began with Mass, celebrated each day in a different rite, followed by the enthroning of the Gospels. Then there were announcements and scheduling matters, so that the actual working sessions did not begin until about 10:15 A.M. each day. The working sessions were mainly given to speeches, first by the cardinals, followed by the bishops, and occasionally by *periti* or other guests. The full roster of scheduled speakers was seldom completed on any given day.

About 11:00 each morning, the scene in the basilica began to resemble that in most houses of parliament or congress as the fathers moved into the coffee bars and cloakrooms nearby to visit and mingle. Loudspeakers there kept everyone informed of the proceedings (which were, after all, being conducted in Latin). When a ballot was announced, the prelates would scurry back to their seats for the vote.

Voting Procedures

In addition to speech making, voting also occurred at these general congregations. The ballots were tabulated by an IBM system designed for this use employing "punch cards" which confused some of the fathers, since many had never seen such ballots before. This led some bishops to cast ballots that were invalid because they were not properly "punched." Modern, high-speed computers were not available but this was a significant improvement over whatever was used in any previous council.

Voting was a key part of the council's process. Votes were taken on a wide variety of levels in the debates and one estimate is that more than 1.5 million ballots were cast during the four sessions of the council. For most matters, a two-thirds majority was needed for passage. The actual voting during the course of the council resulted in vote totals that varied widely. This happened because not all council fathers were present for each vote and, in some cases, ballots were judged invalid due to technical errors on the IBM punch cards.

Voting occurred in the following instances:

A. The general sense of the council fathers regarding their first impressions of a schema, whether or not it should be used as the basis for discussion, was determined by a vote. Many schemata were sent back to the commissions responsible for preparing them for revision before they were even discussed.

B. When disagreement was evident about the general direction a document should take, the matter was placed before the council for a vote, asking "Does it please the fathers that such and such be treated in this or that way?" The outcome of such voting gave direction to the various commissions responsible for incorporating revisions into the various schemata.

C. Specific notions or ideas that might be included in a revision were also voted upon. Sometimes individual words or phrases were considered by vote. They were treated as amendments to the schema. These ideas could be attached to the ballot and sometimes hundreds of them were attached for a single vote, creating major challenges to the commissions and their staffs. These were known in Latin as *juxta modum* votes. With them the council fathers voted yes but with an amendment. Voting on amendments gave direction to the commissions working on the revisions.

D. Voting also occurred to end debate.

E. When documents were nearing acceptability, voting took place again, often resulting in additional amendment suggestions. This voting often took place chapter by chapter or even line by line.

F. When agreement was essentially reached, another penultimate vote was taken in order to send the document to the pope for promulgation.

G. In the special sessions at which documents were actually promulgated by the pope in the presence of the council fathers, a final vote was taken by way of affirmation.

H. Finally, voting took place to bestow honors on
various people or to show support for certain
causes or events.

Applause was not permitted during the proceedings, but
it often occurred and was used as an informal way of
expressing the mind of the fathers on many matters.

A council of presidents was chosen, ten of them, who
would preside in turn over each day's work. Freedom of
speech was assured, but limited to ten minutes and to the
topic at hand. Anyone who strayed from these limits was
gently but firmly interrupted and asked to stay on task or to
end his remarks if they'd grown too long.

The World's Bishops Assert Their Will

The first working session got under way on Saturday, October
13, 1962. The agenda for the day, under the presidency of
Cardinal Tisserant, called for the election of members to the
various commissions that would prepare the schemata for
discussion. These commissions were very important because
they would exercise an editorial influence on council outcomes.
It was to them that the voting was sent and from them that
revised texts were returned to the council for reconsideration.

The plan was that sixteen members would be chosen by
general election in the council for each of ten commissions
while the pope himself would appoint eight more to each
commission.

The council's organizers (the curialists) had proven themselves able to find men for such appointments who generally
agreed with their more cautious approach to church reform.
They intended to present a handpicked slate of "suitable"
candidates to the council fathers at this first session.

Before the election could occur, however, Cardinal
Lienart of Lille, France, in a prepared statement, first moved

that the council participants meet in national or regional caucuses so that they could make a better choice about who should serve in the important commission roles. Cardinal Frings of Cologne gave an immediate second, and this was followed by such vigorous applause that no vote was taken, and after only fifteen minutes in session, the meeting adjourned. The effect of this move was tremendous. The council showed, first of all, that it could act decisively.

Second, the caucusing that followed provided a learning period for all the council fathers because, as lists were drawn up and attempts made to provide for adequate international representation, the discussions were intense. This period fused the participants into a real working body and the outcome was considered by most to be a fair representation of the Church's complexion.

Message to the World

Finally, before the first debate really began, the council published "a message to the world" at the insistence of the pope, whose suggested text was adopted with only minor changes. The message simply proclaimed the Church's desire for the welfare of the human family, both material and spiritual. The cares and needs of the human family were sketched as evidence that men and women need fidelity to the Gospel and to the love of God expressed through Christ. Not a significant document in itself, this message nonetheless set a tone that the world could well understand.

Summary

Many of the characteristics of Vatican II set it apart from previous councils:

The presence of non-Roman Catholic observers, including representatives of the Russian Church for the first time in hundreds of years, was landmark.

The sheer number of participants was staggering compared to past councils. (Vatican I had 800 participants; Vatican II nearly 2,500.)

The truly international flavor was also new for the Church. Most bishops at Vatican I and all previous councils had been European, even those attending from other continents, but this was truly a worldwide body of prelates.

The presence of a press corps, even though not well informed by officials, suggested a new openness and an awareness that the world was watching and listening.

With all these people present, Vatican II was the largest such gathering in the history of the Church.

Vatican II was the first ecumenical council to have electricity, telephones, motorized transportation, typewriters, and computerized voting.

For the first time in history, a council of the whole Church was meeting without the interference of any temporal government. It was the first since the eighth century to meet at a time when there was complete separation of church and state in Italy and south central Europe. This gave the council a more pastoral tone. It removed past political tendencies and pointed to true renewal. And finally, this council's focus on animating the faith of Christians rather than defining doctrine or condemning heretics was also new.

The three cornerstones of the opening of the council seemed to insure that this would, indeed, be a council of reform:

(1) the pope's opening address, offering the world its first hope for true reform of the Roman Catholic Church since the sixteenth century, (2) the active participation in those early elections rather than rubber-stamping a curial list for the commissions, and (3) the gentle, pastoral opening message to the world.

PART TWO: POPE JOHN XXIII's OPENING SPEECH AT THE SECOND VATICAN COUNCIL

October 11, 1962

Paraphrase Text

The entire Church rejoices today
    because that longed-for moment
    has finally arrived when,
        under the watchful eye
        of the Virgin Mother of God,
    the Second Vatican Ecumenical Council is opened,
        here beside the tomb of St. Peter.
The previous ecumenical councils of the Church,
    some twenty in number,
    plus many other regional ones,
    all prove clearly the vigor of the Catholic Church
        and are recorded as shining lights
        in the Church's history.

In calling this particular council,
    I assert once again the Church's enduring authority
    to teach the faith,
    and I hope that in these times,
        filled with needs and opportunities
        as well as errors,
    the Church's teachings will be presented
        exceptionally well
            to all people.
It is natural for us to look back into our history today
    and listen again to the voices of church leadership,
    both in the East and the West,
    where, beginning in the fourth century,
        councils like this have gathered.
But despite the joys of these previous councils,
    there has also been a trail of sorrow and trial,
    just as Simeon foretold to Mary
        that Jesus would be the source
        of both the fall and the rise of many.
What confronts the Church today,
    therefore, is not new:
    those who are in Christ enjoy light,
        goodness,
        order,
        and peace.
Those who oppose Christ sink into confusion,
    bitter human relations,
    and the constant danger of war.
Ecumenical councils like this,
    whenever they gather,
    are an occasion for the celebration once again
        of the unity between Christ
        and the Church.
They lead to a more clear announcement of the truth,

to guidance for people in everyday life,
and to the strengthening of spiritual energy
for goodness's sake.
We now stand in the wake of twenty centuries
of such history as we begin.
For the sake of the historical record,
let me mention the first moment
when the idea of calling such a council came to me.
I first uttered the words on January 25, 1959,
on the feast of the Conversion of St. Paul,
in the church dedicated to him in Rome.
It was completely unexpected,
like a flash of heavenly light,
and it gave rise to three years of tremendous activity
throughout the world
in preparation for this day.
These years alone have been an initial gift of grace.
I confidently trust that under the light of this council
the Church will become richer in spiritual matters
and, with this new energy,
will look to the future without fear.
In fact, by bringing itself up-to-date where needed,
the Church will make people,
families,
and whole nations
really turn their minds toward divine things.
And, therefore, we are all very grateful for this moment.
Moreover, I also want to mention
before you now my own assessment
of the happy circumstances
under which this council begins its work.
As I go about my daily work as pope,
I sometimes have to listen,
with much regret,

to voices of persons who,
though burning with zeal,
are not endowed with too much
sense of discretion or measure.
These people can see nothing but a decline of truth
and the ruin of the Church
in these modern times.
They say that our era, in comparison with past ones,
is getting worse,
and they behave as though they had learned nothing
from history,
which is, nonetheless, the teacher of life.
They behave as though at the time of former councils,
everything was a full triumph
for the Christian idea and religious liberty.
I feel I must disagree with these prophets of gloom
who are always forecasting disaster
as though the end of the world was at hand.
In fact, at the present time,
Divine Providence is leading us
to a new order of human relations which,
by the very effort of the people of this time,
is directed toward the fulfillment
of God's great plans for us.
Everything, even human differences,
leads to a greater good for the Church.
It's easy to see this if you look even casually
through history.
Most of the councils called in the past
were forced to address
serious challenges to the Church
brought about by civil authorities,
even when they thought
they were helping the Church.

Most of the world today
    does not live under such civil tyranny,
    and this is a great thing.
I am saddened, of course,
    by those places where such oppression still exists,
    and indeed, some bishops are noticeable here today
        mainly by their absence
        where they are imprisoned for their faith.
And even though modern life brings with it
    great stress and pressure from economic
        and political sides,
        nonetheless, it at least has the advantage
        of having freed the Church
        from obstacles to its freedom
            in most parts of the world.
The greatest concern of this council is this:
    that the sacred and central truths
    of our Christian faith
        should be guarded and taught
            more effectively.
These central truths embrace the whole human person,
    composed as we are of body and soul,
    and since we're pilgrims on earth,
        they lead us always toward heaven.
This puts into perspective that we are to use earthly things
    only to attain a divine good.
According to the sixth chapter of the Gospel of Matthew,
    Jesus himself called on us to seek first
        the Reign of God,
        addressing our energy to that.
But Jesus also completed that thought by saying that,
    if we did seek that first,
    all worldly things would be given to us
        as well.

Both sides of this equation
    are present in the Church today,
    as they have always been,
        and we take this into account
        as we begin.
In this effort, we will not depart from the truth
    as it is passed on to us
    by the early Fathers and Mothers of the Church.
But we will also be attentive to these times,
    to the new conditions
    and new forms of life
        present in the modern world
        which have opened new arenas of work
            for Catholics.
So while the Church is mindful
    of marvelous human progress,
    it is also eager to remind people
    that God is the true source of wisdom and beauty.
Having said this, it is clear that much is expected of us here
    regarding the passing on of the doctrines
        of the Church,
    as we have done without fail for twenty centuries,
    despite occasional difficulties in that regard.
The important point of this council is not, therefore,
    a discussion of one article or another
    of the fundamental teachings of the Church;
    a council would not be needed for such work.
Instead, the work of this council
    is to better articulate the doctrine of the Church
        for this age.
This doctrine should be studied and expounded
    through the methods of research
    and literary forms of modern thought.
Here is a key distinction on which our work is based:

The substance of our central beliefs is one thing,
and the way in which it is presented is another.
It is this latter presentation of the faith
with which we are concerned here,
and our approach to this
will be a thoroughly pastoral one.
As we open this council we see, as always,
that the truth of Jesus is permanent.
Often, as one age succeeds another,
the opinions of people follow one another
and exclude each other.
Errors creep in, but vanish like fog before the sun.
In the past we have opposed these errors
and often condemned them.
But today we prefer to make use
of the medicine of mercy
rather than that of severity.
We meet the needs of the present day
by demonstrating the validity of our teachings
rather than by condemning others.
In fact, error today is so obvious when it emerges
that people themselves reject it.
People are evermore convinced of the high dignity
of the human person,
the evil of violence,
and the dead end of arms and political domination.
That being so, the Catholic Church in this council
desires to show herself as the loving mother of all:
benign,
patient,
full of mercy and goodness
toward all who are separated from her.
The Church does not offer riches that will pass away
to the people of today.

Like Peter when he was asked for alms,
    we say that we have neither silver nor gold
    but that we have a certain power in Jesus Christ
        to offer the world:
        a way to walk in truth.
We distribute the goods of divine grace to all people,
    and this raises the children of God
        to great dignity.
We open here the fountain of our life-giving doctrines
    which allow all people to understand
    their real dignity and purpose.
Finally, through our members, we spread Christian charity,
    the most powerful tool
        in eliminating the seeds of discord
        and in establishing harmony,
            peace,
            and unity.
True peace and salvation are associated with having
    a complete grasp of revealed truth.
This truth is passed on
    through the doctrines of the Church,
    and the Church wishes very much
        to promote and defend this truth
        so that everyone can have access to it
        with a unity of understanding.
Unfortunately, the whole Christian family does not have
    this unity of mind.
The Catholic Church considers it a duty to work actively
    to bring about that unity,
    which Jesus himself called for
        in his final prayers.
It is a triple sort of unity which we seek.
First, a unity among Catholics themselves
    which we want to keep firm and strong.

Second, a unity of prayer and desire
 among those other Christians
 now separated from Rome.
And third, a unity in esteem and respect
 for those who follow non-Christian religions.
It is the clear aim of this council
 to bring together the Church's best energies
 and to strive to have people welcome more favorably
  the good tidings of salvation.
This council will prepare and consolidate the path
 toward that unity of humankind
 which is required as a necessary foundation
  in order that the earthly city
  may be brought to resemble the heavenly one
   where truth reigns,
   charity is the law,
   and eternity is the timetable.
In conclusion, I direct my voice to you,
 my venerable fellow bishops of the Church.
We are gathered here today
 in this great Vatican Basilica
 upon which the history of the Church is hinged,
  where heaven and earth are closely joined,
  near the tomb of Peter
   and so many others
   who have gone before us in faith.
The council now beginning rises in the Church
 like daybreak,
 a forerunner of most splendid light.
It is now only dawn.
 And already,
 at this first announcement of the rising day,
  how much sweetness fills our heart!
Everything here breathes sanctity

and arouses great joy.
The Church is now in your hands,
gathered as you are here
from all the continents of the world.
We might say that heaven and earth
are united in the holding of this council,
the saints of heaven to protect us
and the people on earth
looking for inspiration and guidance.
Indeed, our work is expected to correspond
to the modern needs
of the various peoples of the world.
This requires of you serenity of mind,
brotherly concord,
moderation in proposals,
dignity in discussion,
and wisdom of deliberation.
God grant that your labors and work,
toward which the eyes of all people
and desires of the entire world
are turned,
may generously fulfill the hopes of all.
Almighty God!
In you we place all our confidence,
not trusting in our own strength.
Look down kindly on these pastors of your Church.
May the light of your grace help us
in making decisions
and in making laws.
Graciously hear the prayers which we offer you
with unanimity of faith, voice, and mind.
O Mary, help of Christians,
help of bishops,
arrange all things for a happy and helpful outcome.

With your spouse, St. Joseph;
    the holy apostles, Peter and Paul;
      St. John the Baptist; and St. John the Evangelist,
        intercede to God for us.
Jesus Christ, our loving redeemer,
    immortal ruler of people and the ages,
      be love,
      be power,
      and be glory for ever and ever. Amen.

PART THREE: THE MESSAGE OF THE SECOND VATICAN COUNCIL TO THE WORLD

October 20, 1962

Paraphrase Text

We wish to convey to all people and to all nations
    the message of salvation, love, and peace
    which we have received from Jesus Christ.
In fact, that is the very reason we have gathered here,
    we who form one apostolic body
      with the successor of Peter.
Under the guidance of the Holy Spirit,
    we intend to renew ourselves
    and to become better witnesses of the Gospel.
We strive to offer the people of this age
    the truth of God in a pure form,
    so they can understand it and accept it freely.
We believe in Jesus Christ,
    that God loves us greatly,
    that Jesus freed us from the slavery of sin,

and that all things are reconciled in him.
Moreover, we also receive the Holy Spirit
    to allow us to love God
    and share unity in Christ.
Therefore, we are not strangers
    to earthly concerns
    since we are called to live as sisters and brothers.
The Church's task is not to dominate life
    but to serve it.
And while we hope the faith may shine more clearly
    because of the work of this council,
    we also expect an impetus for human welfare
        to result from our work.
We mean by this that we hope to encourage
    the findings of science,
    the progress of the arts and technology,
    and a greater expansion of culture.
United here from every nation on earth,
    we are keenly aware of people's anxieties,
    their sorrows and desires and hopes,
        especially those who are poor and weak
        or suffering from hunger,
            misery,
            or ignorance.
There are two challenges that stand squarely before us.
First, there is no woman or man on earth
    who does not hate war
    and long for world peace,
        and this is also the greatest wish
        of the Church.
The Church has long called for this peace
    and admirably represents the whole world,

a true diversity of races,
    nations,
    and tongues.
We proclaim that all men and women
    are sisters and brothers
    irrespective of the race or nation
        to which they belong.
Second, we deeply desire social justice
    for the world,
    and we understand ourselves to be needed today
        to denounce injustice
        and to restore the true order of goods
        so that all may live with dignity.
Therefore, we humbly and ardently invite all
    to collaborate with us
    to establish in the world
        a more ordered way of living
        and greater sister and brotherhood.
We invite all,
    not only those who are Catholic
    but all who believe in Christ
        and all people of goodwill.
In fact, it is the divine will
    that the Reign of God,
    expressed through charity
    is present here and now, in a sense,
        in anticipation of the eternal bliss.
It is our ardent and only desire
    that the light of Christ may shine in the world!

The Council Itself

Chapter Four

❖

PART ONE: HOW TO APPROACH
CHURCH DOCUMENTS

*C*hurch documents have authority
   based on a certain hierarchy
   and defined by several factors.
Decretal letters and constitutions rank very high.
A decretal letter is used to declare an infallible doctrine
   or to pronounce the canonization of a saint.
A constitution is used to declare a teaching
   that is of a substantial nature,
   one that is central to the entire Church.
Also at a higher rank are papal bulls,
   motu proprios,
   and encyclicals.
A papal bull,
   named after its red seal, or *bulla* in Italian,
   is a very solemn pronouncement,
      used to convoke Vatican II, for example,
      and to declare certain doctrines.
A *motu proprio* is a rather personal papal decree,
   written by the pope himself,
   signed in his own hand, and
   used to declare the rules for the council, for example,
      or to make papal appointments.
An encyclical is somewhat lower in rank,
   used to declare the social and moral teachings
      of the Church.

(There were no encyclicals issued
    as official documents of Vatican II.)

Significantly lower in rank yet
    are addresses and papal speeches
        used to give the opinion of the pope
        or to make an announcement.
At about that same rank are decrees and declarations,
    of which there were a total of twelve at Vatican II.

A decree gives a significant teaching
    but one that requires further discussion,
    while a declaration usually addresses an area
        that may be, by its nature, controversial
        and in need of further doctrinal development.
Close in rank to these are instructions,
    used to amplify other documents
    and give specific steps to carry them out.
Below these at various levels of rank
    are the opinions of the Roman Curia
        and other prelates.
Documents published by a council
    are considered very authoritative
    because they're prepared by such a wide consultation
        and because they reflect the current Church.
But another factor in measuring their relative authority
    is how theologically trained men and women
    receive them and understand them.
A certain bishop may publish a pastoral letter,
    for example,
    which is so profound and is received so well
        that it gains much authority.
On the other hand,
    a particular pronouncement at a higher rank

may seem to the faithful who hear it
    to be out of touch
    or not in accord with their consciences.
With this in mind,
    the documents of Vatican II seem to hold
    a variety of places in the post-Vatican II Church.
The four constitutions from the council
    are very well received,
        very strong,
        very influential.
Likewise the decree on ecumenism,
        and the declarations on religious liberty
        and on the relationship of the Church
            to non-Christian religions.
These latter three are really documents of historic impact
    and long-lasting influence.
Others are moderately influential,
    though not earthshaking,
    and some are considered weaker,
        having less influence
        and in need of further development.
And finally, a couple are seen not to be in the spirit
    of the council's overall theology at all.

Furthermore, these documents are committee creations,
    filled with compromise
    and competing theologies.
One could argue, for example,
    that at least four theologies of the Church
    run through the constitution on the Church.

In fact, it seems to have been a deliberate method
    for the writers of these documents
    to use ambiguous language
        that could be acceptable to all.

It seems intentional on their part
  that these documents would be "catholic,"
  which means they would reach widely
    to embrace many people.
Doing this made it possible at the council
  to encourage large majorities to approve them,
  which gave them moral force later.
But it's also in the very nature of being catholic
  that the embrace would be wide.

This leaves room in the documents
  for some discussion and "midrash" on the texts,
  and it seems to imply that this process
    would go on and on.
It suggests that the council did not see itself
  as the final word on these questions
  but rather as the force which opened the Church
    to the times,
      opened the Church
  to the methods of study and adaptation
  for which the times call.
"Midrash" is a method of commenting
  on certain sacred writings
  by comparing them with other sections
    of the same text
    or with other similar material.
Used mainly by Jews but also by Christians,
  midrash employs stories,
  metaphors,
  the sayings of wise church leaders,
  and the opinions of various religious people.
It's an important method of coming to understand,
    internalize,
    and witness to
      key sacred writings and ideas.

These documents are filled with sections,
     phrases,
     and whole theological thoughts
          that beg for a midrashic approach.
Most of them can't be quoted as proof
     that this or that should be done in the Church,
     although they're sometimes used that way
          by people who would never do that
          with Scripture.
They beg to be discussed,
     argued over,
     debated,
     and even, kindly, disagreed about.
          By all of us.
An example from chapter two
     of the decree on ecumenism will illustrate this:
"Christ summons the Church
     as she goes her pilgrim way
     to that continual reformation
          of which she always has need
          insofar as she is an institution of humans
               here on earth.
Therefore, if the influence of events or of the times
     has led to deficiencies
          in conduct,
          in church discipline,
          or even in the language of its doctrine
          (which must be carefully distinguished
               from the deposit of Faith),
     these should be appropriately corrected
          when the time is right to do so."

What does it mean that "if the influence . . . of the times
     has led to deficiencies . . .
     in Church discipline . . .

these should be appropriately corrected
when the time is right"?
Does this mean we can discuss issues before us
with the hope that, if there's agreement,
they might be corrected?
And what does it mean that the Church
is in constant need of reformation?
Even the use of that term *reformation*
summons images of Luther, Calvin, and Zwingli
calling the Church to reform!
(The word in the Latin original is, indeed,
reformationem.)
Midrash on this one, single text
could last for a generation!

The Church longs for a fresh word today,
and the world longs for the Church
to find its voice.
I believe that these documents,
when read more like Scripture than theology,
can be the basis for that.
If we take them seriously
and read them alongside the lectionary,
we will need no catechisms.
We will find in them what we seek,
what the world seeks,
that fresh voice leading us for today.

And then, just as the Scriptures are proclaimed as
"The Word of the Lord,"
so these texts would be proclaimed as
"The Word of the Church."

PART TWO: A CHRONOLOGICAL OUTLINE OF ALL MAJOR EVENTS AT THE SECOND VATICAN COUNCIL

THE PERIOD BEFORE THE COUNCIL,
October 1958 to September 1962

- October 28, 1958: **Angelo Roncalli** is elected Pope John XXIII.
- January 25, 1959: **Pope John XXIII announces his intention to call the council,** along with a synod in the Diocese of Rome and a revision of the code of canon law. His announcement is met with little support by curialists. (See paraphrase of this announcement, p. 65.)
- June 18, 1959: Just six months later, Pope John sets in motion **the needed preparations** indicating his intention to move forward, despite objections from some of his staff. The pope seeks advice and suggestions from 2,594 members of the world's hierarchy in 134 nations. More than 80 percent of them participate.
- June 5, 1960, Pentecost Sunday: **Pope John issues** a ***motu proprio*** announcing the formation of various commissions which will prepare the documents for debate in the council sessions. (See lists of commissions and their presidents, Appendix Two.)
- December 25, 1961: **Pope John issues** a ***bull*** formally convoking the Second Vatican Council.
- February 5, 1962: **Pope John sets the opening date of the council** for October 11, 1962, the feast of the Divine Maternity of Mary. In so doing, he ties this council to the memory of the Council of Ephesus in 431, which defined

the doctrine of Mary as the *Theotokos*, which means "Mother of God."

✳ July 20, 1962: Invitations are sent to **separated Christians** encouraging them to send observers to the council.

✳ September 5, 1962 (only five weeks before the opening): **Pope John issues a *motu proprio*** naming the heads of the ten council commissions which will oversee the preparation and presentation of the official schemata or discussion draft documents to be considered by the council. He also spells out the council's rules and procedures and names a presiding council of ten cardinals from nine nations who will take turns presiding over council activities when the pope himself is not present. (See list of council presidents, Appendix Two.)

Among the rules is one that required a two-thirds majority for enactment of council pronouncements. The pope wishes to have as much unanimity as possible in council outcomes to add moral force to them. He invites non-Catholic observers not only to the solemn public sessions but also to the working sessions in which all the bishops will participate.

✳ September 11, 1962: **Pope John addresses the world,** asking for prayers for the council.

THE FIRST SESSION
October to December 1962

✳ October 11, 1962: **The opening session gets under way.** (See paraphrase of John XXIII's opening speech, p. 85.) The first session runs until December 8, 1962.

✳ October 13, 1962:   The council meets in its first general congregation but adjourns after only an hour, following **the motion by Cardinal Lienart** (Lille), seconded by Cardinal Frings (Cologne), to allow the national groups time to meet to consider who would best be chosen for the 160 posts open in the ten commissions which would steer the council debates. The motion meets with approval by acclamation and the session adjourns before 10:00 A.M. This is seen as a blow to the conservatives at the council who had hoped to have their handpicked choices for these seats approved.

(The "conservative party" at the council was composed of council fathers from many parts of the world, including many working in the Curia, the congregations and offices that assist the pope in the worldwide administration of the Church. These were generally opposed to the reforms being proposed because they believed the Church was adequately meeting the demands of the Gospel in its pre-Vatican II form.)

On the same day, at about the same hour, more than eight hundred journalists are attempting to enter St. Peter's as all the council fathers are pouring out, causing confusion for all. (**The journalists met that morning with Pope John,** who urged them to present the proceedings fairly and accurately and promised cooperation with them. He urged them to avoid the sensational and to report on the substantial aspects of the council. "We felt keenly that we must tell you personally how much we desire your loyal cooperation in presenting this great event in its true colors," he told them.)

On the same day, the pope also speaks to the thirty-five delegate-observers and guests representing **seventeen**

Orthodox and Protestant denominations. (See list of denominations represented here, Appendix Two.)

"It is now for the Catholic Church to bend herself to her work with calmness and generosity," he tells them. "It is for you to observe her with renewed and friendly attention."

※ October 16, 1962: **The schema on Liturgy** is chosen as the first item with which the council will deal. The council fathers pass over other possible schemata because they seem unready.

※ October 20, 1962: **The council's first act** is to send a "message to the world," calling for peace and social justice for all humankind. "We wish to convey to all people and to all nations the message of salvation, love, and peace which Jesus Christ, Son of the Living God, brought to the world and entrusted to the Church," the message begins. (See paraphrase of this message, p. 95.)

※ October 22, 1962: **The schema** (draft document) **on Liturgy is introduced** for debate. The press office reports that this is the first topic because the council's work will be directed primarily toward the task of the internal renewal of the Church. The debate is wide-ranging, including suggestions for use of the vernacular, more varied use of Scripture, communion under both forms, and concelebration. The discussion on the Liturgy lasts through fifteen general sessions, ending on November 13. The council fathers propose 625 amendments to the original schema. It eventually meets with their overwhelming approval, a blow for the conservatives at the council.

※ October 31, 1962: **The bishops of the United States establish twelve committees** to guide them and their work by studying various issues coming before the council and by advising them on their implications for the Church in the United States.

✵ November 14, 1962: **The schema on sources of divine revelation** is introduced for debate under the name "The Twofold Source of Revelation."

The schema on Liturgy undergoes its first major vote to determine whether, in substance, it adequately represents what the council fathers want. It passes with a mere forty-six negative votes! This is a major victory for the progressive party, and a clear sign to the waiting world that this council will indeed undertake real reform and not simply affirm the status quo.

✵ November 20, 1962: **The debate on divine revelation** is halted amid a growing consensus that the schema as originally presented does not adequately address the needs of the day or the spirit of Pope John in calling the council in the first place. "What, then, did the pope have in mind?" Cardinal Bea, the feeble but brilliant leader of the Secretariat for Promoting Christian Unity, asks. He had in mind, the cardinal says, "that the faith of the Church should be presented in all its integrity and purity, but in such a manner that it will be received today with goodwill. For we are shepherds. . . . What our times demand is a pastoral approach," he goes on to say, "demonstrating the love and kindness that flow from our religion." It is Cardinal Bea's voice but the sentiments of John XXIII, and everyone knows it.

A vote is taken to determine whether the schema as it stands should be returned to its drafting commission for revisions. The vote fails to reach the two-thirds majority required by the rules, but in a historic move, Pope John himself intervenes and the schema is sent to a specially designed commission for revision. This is another blow for the conservatives at the council.

✳ November 23, 1962: The schema on **the modern means of communications** for preaching the Gospel to all and spreading the principles of justice, peace, and human dignity is introduced.

✳ November 26, 1962: **The schema on communications** is essentially approved as it stands. Work is taken up on what are considered more important matters, including the matter of promoting unity between Roman and Eastern Christians.

✳ November 27, 1962: **The first lay observer** is invited to the council. He is Jean Guitton, a member of the French Academy whom Pope John knew when he lived in Paris as papal nuncio to France.

✳ November 30, 1962: **The schema on the unity of Roman and Eastern Churches** is defeated 2,068 to 36, with eight invalid ballots. The matter will be addressed again later.

✳ December 1, 1962: **The schema on the Church is introduced** for debate by Cardinal Alfredo Ottaviani, chair of the Theological Commission which had prepared it. By and large, Ottaviani's commission has prepared a draft that hails the status quo as acceptable and does not address the Church as the People of God.

✳ December 4, 1962: **Cardinal Suenens** speaks in favor of redrafting **the schema on the Church.** As Vatican I was the council of the papacy, he says, let this be the council of the Church of Christ, light of nations! He goes on to propose that the document be divided into two parts: one dealing with the nature of the Church as the Mystical Body and the other dealing with the Church's mission in the world. He calls on the Church to be in dialogue with the society around it on matters such as the dignity of the human person, social justice, private property, the poor, internal peace within nations, and international relations. His speech is met with sustained applause, so much so that it has to be choked off by the day's president with a reminder that such boisterous responses are not in order.

Cardinal Bea seconds Suenens's remarks, followed by others who agree, along with a smaller number who favor the approach taken by Ottaviani's commission.

✳ December 5, 1962:   **Cardinal Giovanni Battista Montini of Milan** rises to take the microphone. In the entire first session he addresses the council only twice. He says that he approves wholeheartedly of Cardinal Suenens's statement of the day before regarding the need for revision of the document on the Church and confirms the suspicion in the council that Suenens has indeed been speaking the mind and heart of the pope himself. The Church, Montini goes on to say, is nothing by itself. It is not so much that the Church has Christ, he says, but that Christ has the Church to carry on his work of bringing salvation to all. It is up to this council, he says, to clearly restate "the mind and will of Christ" by defining collegiality among bishops, projecting a truly ecumenical view of the Church, and teaching faithfully that each bishop is indeed a vicar of Christ. It is necessary, he says, to send this schema back to its commission for redrafting. All present know that he is speaking for Pope John. (Montini is the only cardinal from outside Rome who has been invited to reside in the papal apartments during the eight weeks of the first session.)

Only a few months later, this very cardinal, Montini, is named Paul VI.

※ December 6, 1962: Pope John orders that, between sessions, all **the schemata are to be reworked** by various commissions and sent to the bishops of the world for their comment. To coordinate this effort, he is creating a new central commission, which will include Cardinals Lienart, Urbani, Spellman, Confalonieri, Dopfner, and Suenens. The pope orders the commission to consult theological experts on a wide scale. All of this is yet another serious setback for the conservatives at the council.

※ December 7, 1962: The council approves **the first chapter of the document on the Liturgy** with 1,922 yes votes, 180 "yes with reservations" votes, 11 no votes, and 5 invalid ballots. The chapter allows certain changes with which to update the Mass, including the use of vernacular languages and a more participatory rite. The chapter contains the fundamental principles which the following chapters will implement. The Church's sacramental and prayer life is moved to center stage in this act, but it is a blow for the conservatives at the council.

Pope John visits the council for the first time since its opening to thank the members for their work and for their generosity and kindness toward one another.

※ December 8, 1962: **The first session of the Second Vatican Council is formally adjourned** for nine months, until September 8, 1963. In his address, the pope stresses that he appreciates the sometimes sharply divergent views expressed in the first session because this demonstrates the "holy liberty" of thought in the Church. "A good beginning has been made," he says.

The first session has produced no completed results.

The Period Between Sessions 1 and 2

December 1962 to September 1963

- June 3, 1963: **Pope John XXIII dies.**
- June 21, 1963: **Pope Paul VI is elected.**
- June 22, 1963: **Pope Paul announces his intention to continue the ecumenical council.** He announces the reopening date as September 29, 1963, sooner than had been expected by even the most optimistic observer since preparations had stopped upon the death of Pope John.
- June 23, 1963: From the window of the papal library, Pope Paul introduces his friend and confidant **Cardinal Suenens** to a cheering crowd.
- September 15, 1963: Pope Paul announces the formation of **a steering committee** to direct the work of the second session. The members of the committee are three progressives (Cardinals Suenens, Dopfner, and Lercaro) and one moderate (Agagianian).
- September 21, 1963: **Pope Paul delivers an address to members of the Curia** and other Vatican workers in which he clearly and tactfully expresses every theme of reform that had been raised by the progressives at the first session. He calls on the Curia to be faithful to his wishes and makes himself perfectly clear by referring to himself as "the pope who today has made the legacy of Pope John his own and has also made it a program for the entire Church." He discusses the need to update the Curia itself by using Pope John's word, *aggiornamento*, and then says, simply, "Various reforms are therefore necessary."

THE SECOND SESSION
September to December 1963

✳ September 29, 1963: **The second session of the council opens.** Pope Paul has invited sixty-three separated Christian observers and eleven laymen to attend this session, an increase over the first session. The pope opens this session with a long and stirring speech, addressing the "living presence" of Pope John and committing himself to continued reform.

In his opening address, Pope Paul states his four main goals for the council as the following:

(1) To raise the understanding of ourselves as the Church, including a precise definition of the nature of the Church as mystery. The first question he raises is the place of the bishops therein and their relationship to the papacy, which is the question known by the term *collegiality*.

(2) To reform the Church, especially the Liturgy, but not to turn the life of the Church upside down.

(3) To bring together all Christians in unity. The pope calls the process of reestablishing Christian unity the council's "spiritual drama."

(At this point he turns to the separated Christians seated within his sight and says to them, "If we are in any way to blame for this separation, we humbly beg God's forgiveness and ask pardon, too, of our brethren who feel they have been injured by us. For our part, we willingly forgive the injuries which the Catholic Church has suffered.")

(4) To engage in dialogue with the contemporary world. The pope says that the council fathers are no longer concerned with only their own limited affairs but rather with those of the world. The pope adds that the council fathers no longer want to conduct a dialogue among themselves, but rather to open one with the world. About this dialogue, he says, "we ought to be realists."

※ October 1, 1963: The council takes up **the debate on the Church** once again with the overwhelming approval of the assembly. The vote to proceed on the basis of the revised schema is 2,231 to 43, with 27 invalid ballots. The revised schema includes a greater emphasis on the Church as mystery, on the Church first and foremost as the People of God, and other changes desired by the council fathers.

※ October 4–28, 1963: The debate on chapter two of **the schema on the Church** begins with a discussion of collegiality which lasts for ten days. Among other debated points are the following: (1) whether to include a chapter on Mary in the document on the Church or to have a separate document devoted to her; (2) the nature of the Church; (3) the role and place of the laity; (4) the reinstitution of a permanent and possibly married diaconate; (5) ecumenical questions; (6) the relationship of church and state; (7) the universal call to holiness; (8) religious orders; and others.

The overall discussion on this document lasts twenty-three days and is characterized by rather long, somewhat dull and repetitious speeches. But even after this long debate, no final document is in sight because the revisions will have to come from the Theological Commission, headed by Cardinal Ottaviani. He is convening the commission only once each week, and sometimes less often. It gradually becomes clear that the pace of revision will be extremely slow, which frustrates the council fathers and causes some to return to their home dioceses.

Clearly, Cardinal Ottaviani does not consider speeches on the council floor as having any legislative force. It is equally clear that any outcomes might take several years to be finalized, dashing the hopes of those who want reform more quickly. **A crisis** is under way in the council as these sentiments of despair take hold.

❈ October 22, 1963:   Cardinal Suenens urges that the number of laypeople present at the council be increased and that **the number should include women.** "Unless I am mistaken," he says, "women make up one-half of the world's population."

❈ October 23, 1963:   **A summit meeting of council leaders** is held to try to move the stalled council, but little progress is reported. The next day, it is announced that the following Monday, October 28, no general session of the council will be held. Instead, Pope Paul will say a special Mass in memory of Pope John. Cardinal Suenens will give the address. On the Sunday evening before this, Cardinal Suenens and Pope Paul dine privately together. Meanwhile the debate and the standoff between Cardinal Ottaviani and the progressives continues.

❈ October 24, 1963:   Dr. Edmund Schlink of the University of Heidelberg and the Evangelical (Lutheran) Church of Germany speaks on behalf of most of the separated and Orthodox Christians in saying that **the document on the Church** is defective because it gives no recognition to churches not in communion with Rome. "It appears," he says, "more Roman than catholic."

※ October 28, 1963: The 8:30 A.M. Mass is celebrated as planned with Pope Paul presiding. After Mass, **Cardinal Suenens approaches the pulpit,** appearing calm and serious. He carefully takes out his glasses and puts them on. He unfolds his notes, pauses, and looks at Pope Paul, who is seated on his throne. Then he begins his speech. He speaks in French, a significant departure from the Latin of the council. He has also distributed copies of his text in other languages to be certain he is heard by all. Although he does not mention the crisis explicitly, his speech is clearly an attempt to move the council forward and it is clear as well that he is speaking for the pope. He recalls the memory of John XXIII, quoting his very words: "We have no reason to be afraid. Fear comes only from a lack of faith." He ends by calling the council to its task of making the Gospel understandable in today's world. Long applause greets his speech. He leaves the pulpit and approaches the throne of the pope, who is smiling broadly. He bends and kisses his ring. Then the pope rises and embraces him, embracing as well his words. A second round of applause fills the basilica.

※ October 30, 1963: Cardinal Suenens, frustrated by the lack of progress and the continued stalling tactics of the curialists, has (on October 15) offered the council **five proposals,** asking for a vote to determine the mind of the council on the place of bishops in the Church. The curialists consider this "illegal" because the proposals have not come from them. On **October 30, a vote is taken.** The overwhelming outcome supports the progressive position.

※ October 29 to November 7, 1963: The debate on **the document on the Church** continues amid claims from Cardinal Ottaviani that the voting, which had occurred on October 30 and which showed overwhelming support for the progressive (and papal) point of view, was not binding. Furthermore, open accusations are made that the schema is being altered in ways not approved by the assembly. Open calls are made to reduce the prominence of the Curia.

Despite the intervention of Suenens and the pope, the stagnation continues. The attacks grow more biting and more and more personal in nature. There is a growing feeling that the Church's administrators in the Curia are acting like legislators, a role belonging solely to the bishops.

❊ November 8, 1963:   **Cardinal Frings of Cologne** speaks in favor of the reform of the Curia, saying that the members of the Curia must not confuse administrative roles with legislative ones. The methods and behavior of the members of the Curia, he says, do not conform at all to the modern era and are a cause of scandal to the world. He is referring mainly to the judgmental approach of the Holy Office, headed by Cardinal Ottaviani, and to the secret proceedings of the Italy office against many theologians. His remarks are met with loud and long applause, even though that is forbidden in the debates.

Shaking with anger and emotion, **Cardinal Ottaviani responds** that in criticizing the Holy Office, one attacks the pope himself. He goes on to claim that his commission is the only group that can define collegiality. His remarks, too, are met with applause. This exchange brings the debate into the open and is clearly the most dramatic debate of the council to this date as the "new order" of collegiality of bishops is juxtaposed with the "old order."

On the same day, in another unrelated but important matter, a communiqué is issued regarding **the attitude of**

Catholics toward non-Christians, especially the Jews. The paper states clearly that the Jews are not guilty for the death of Jesus and calls for respect and mutual understanding.

✳ November 18, 1963: **The schema on ecumenism** is introduced for debate. The document is largely hailed as both sound in doctrine and pastorally oriented. It generates great enthusiasm on the floor of the council, in part because of Cardinal Bea's tireless efforts as head of the Secretariat for Promoting Christian Unity. Cardinal Bea's report on the matter is listened to reverently and greeted with an ovation. At one point, Cardinal Leger of Canada says, "The present hope for and movement toward unity are not passing impulses, but are inspired by the Gospel and the Holy Spirit." Only a small number of conservatives oppose the schema. One of them, Cardinal Ruffini, speaks at the November 29 debate, expressing the conservatives' view that the Roman Catholic Church has nothing to learn and nothing to be sorry for. "We strongly hope," he says, "that our separated brethren will again embrace the Catholic Church of Rome." Dialogue, he says, has only one purpose: to "bring back" those in error to the real Church. In the end, it becomes clear that this is a minority point of view.

Initially, a draft document on religious liberty is included in this schema and reported to the council by Bishop De Smedt of Belgium. Religious liberty is defined as "the right to free exercise of religion according to the dictates of conscience. Looked at negatively," the report goes on, "it means immunity from outside coercion."

✳ November 21, 1963: Pope Paul **enlarges the commissions** with an eye to expediting their work and forestalling the delaying tactics of the conservatives.

- November 22, 1963: **The document providing for the sweeping reform of the Liturgy** is approved at 12:05 P.M. by the council fathers. The vote to send this document to Pope Paul for promulgation is an overwhelming 2,159 to 19. Prolonged applause greets the announcement of the vote.

  President John Kennedy is assassinated in the United States at about 7:00 P.M., Roman time, sending a hush upon the whole city.

  One news commentator writes that in a single year, two great Catholic men died, Pope John XXIII and the president of the United States, having initiated much work which they left unfinished.

- November 25, 1963: **The document on communications media** is approved by the council fathers by a vote of 1,598 to 503. The large negative vote results from a widespread sense in the council that, while this matter might merit some attention, it is not worthy of the actions of a council. This document is seen as out of step with other council outcomes, reflecting a view of the press that is unrealistic. (It may have been that Pope Paul allowed the document to pass as it did in order to move it off the council's agenda and to get on to more important work.)

- December 1, 1963: Cardinal Bea graciously sums up the council **debate on ecumenism** and promises to give the recommendations of the council fathers careful consideration in revising the schema for the third session.

- December 3, 1963: **A petition,** signed by two hundred council fathers from forty-six nations, asking for a special schema to condemn Communism, Marxism, and Socialism, is presented to the papal secretary of state. (No such schema ever reached the council floor.)

Two laymen address the council to support the movement toward ecumenism and the expanding role of laypeople in the Church. They are Jean Guitton of France and Vittorino Veronese of Italy.

✳ December 4, 1963: **The second session of the Second Vatican Council closes** with a solemn liturgy and the promulgation of the constitution on the Liturgy and the decree on communications media. Voting on them is as follows:

> **Liturgy:** 2,147 to 4
> **Communications:** 1,960 to 164

There is a general sense that progress in this session has been slow, as it had been in the first session. Pope Paul also takes this occasion to announce his plan to visit the Holy Land between sessions. The date for the third session is set for September 14, 1964.

THE PERIOD BETWEEN SESSIONS 2 AND 3
December 1963 to September 1964

✳ January 1964: **Pope Paul VI** (who is the bishop of Rome) **and Patriarch Athenagoras I** (who is the bishop of Constantinople) meet in a historic gesture of reconciliation in the Holy Land while both are on pilgrimage there. They meet three times, first at the pope's place of residence in the Holy Land where he greets the patriarch with the gift of a chalice and says that he hopes they will one day share it again. The second meeting is at the patriarch's place of residence in the Holy Land where the pope receives the gift of a pectoral chain, symbolic of a bishop's apostolic succession, which he immediately dons. The third meeting is an accidental one on the street, where they stand for ten minutes of intimate visiting.

This carefully planned meeting, the first between the pope and the patriarch since the Middle Ages, results in a major move forward in relations between the Churches of the East and the West and lays the groundwork for work still to be done on the document on ecumenism, which is on the agenda for the third session of the council.

THE THIRD SESSION
September to November 1964

※ September 14, 1964: **The third session opens** with a concelebrated Mass in St. Peter's. Pope Paul's opening remarks are a call to the council fathers to define the place of the bishop in the Church, an effort which has thus far proved to be frustrating for the council fathers because of the tactics the Curia members have used to prevent any reduction in their powers.

※ September 15, 1964: **New rules** are announced which are generally seen to benefit the conservative minority and the curialist party. In general, they are designed (1) to limit the activity of theological experts, known as *periti*, who are working with the bishops and (2) to prevent the distribution of "unauthorized" documents.

※ September 16, 1964: A vote is taken on chapter one of **the document on the Church**: 2,189 favor it, 11 oppose it, and 63 vote "yes with reservations." This chapter provides the important principles about the nature of the Church. The remainder of the document rests on these principles.

※ September 18, 1964: Four votes are taken on various articles composing chapter two of **the document on the**

Church: the voting runs overwhelmingly in favor of this chapter, averaging 2,128 in favor and 39 opposed. This chapter defines the Church as the People of God.

✳ September 21, 1964: Voting begins on various parts of chapter three of **the document on the Church** and continues through eight council workdays. The voting is overwhelmingly in favor of collegiality, with only a small minority continuing to oppose the concept. This chapter, as Pope Paul pointed out in his opening address for the third session, forms the core work of this council. Vatican I had defined only the primacy of the papacy and the doctrine of infallibility. The work on collegiality being done in Vatican II, in a sense, completes the unfinished work of Vatican I. The minority members see this move as dangerous because they fear it will weaken the role of the Curia, which they believe is solely capable of governing the Church. On September 21 as the voting begins, Archbishop Pietro Parente, thought to be a conservative on this issue, announces his support for the notion of collegiality, urging the council fathers not to fear that a breakdown of the Church will result. (The minority curialists are predicting such a breakdown.) His support proves to be a fatal blow to the hope of the curialists to resist collegiality.

✳ September 23, 1964 The debate on **the declaration on religious liberty** is opened. Father John Courtney Murray, S.J., an American *peritus*, is largely responsible for this document, which the majority at the council, including those from the United States, strongly support.

Eight women religious and seven lay unmarried women are named as auditors at the council. (See list of women auditors, Appendix Two.) In his opening speech for this session, the pope has said, "And we are delighted to welcome among the auditors our beloved daughters in Christ, the first women in history to participate in a conciliar assembly."

- September 28, 1964: **The declaration on the Jews** is presented for debate in the council. The debate produces a statement more inclusive of Moslems and other non-Christians in addition to a more strongly worded and clearly stated passage ending the notion that the Jews are somehow guilty for the death of Jesus, a charge known as "deicide." (The term *deicide*, which refers to the idea that the Jews had killed Jesus, was the basis of most persecution of the Jews throughout the centuries.)

- September 30, 1964: **The schema on divine revelation** is presented for debate. The majority of council fathers favor its approach to Scripture, which is in keeping with the modern biblical movement, including the encyclicals of Pope Pius XII on the matter: *Divino Afflante Spiritu* in 1943 and *Humani Generis* in 1951. This modern movement allows for the application of new methods of research and new understandings of history in coming to terms with the meaning of the sacred texts.

- October 6, 1964: **The schema on the lay apostolate** is presented for debate. Most council fathers see it as clerical in tone, as though the role of the laity is to "assist" the clergy, using the Catholic Action Movement as its basis. (The 1917 code of canon law had defined a layperson as "one who is not a cleric.")

It is also seen as lacking a solid theological basis in the sacrament of baptism. Furthermore, although the document deals with the laity, no laity had been consulted on it until the last minute. Bishop Alexander Carter of Canada says that the document is "conceived in the sin of clericalism."

Archbishop D'Souza of India says that it is high time to treat the laity like "grown-ups. Laymen must be treated as brothers by the clergy," he says.

※ October 9, 1964:   Cardinal Suenens calls for a broader definition of the role of the laity in the Church before continuing the debate on the document dealing with them.

※ October 12, 1964:   **An "October Crisis"** threatens the council. In an effort to bury the document on the Jews and the one on religious liberty, the conservative curialists, through the pen of Archbishop Felici, attempt to derail the progress of the two documents. He sends a letter to Cardinal Bea, head of the secretariat responsible for their preparation, requiring that he submit these documents to the conservatively oriented Theological Commission for revision. In his letter, Felici suggests he is speaking for the pope. Despite the well-known efforts of the conservative minority to control the outcome of the council, this bold demand stuns everyone. The leaders of the majority meet to respond. In firm and concise language, they draft an appeal to the pope, asking him for clarification. The pope, in turn, assures them that these two documents will indeed remain under Cardinal Bea's jurisdiction, but he strikes a compromise by allowing the Theological Commission to "examine" the documents.

When the letter from the progressives to the pope is released, the whole affair boils over into the press, and the official Vatican newspaper heavily criticizes the press for publishing it. Clearly, the modern Church has to learn the ways of the news media as well as those of Christian charity in order to do its work.

(The letter to the pope asking for an intervention begins with the Latin words *magno cum dolore*, with great sorrow, which historians have said characterized the entire third session due to the wranglings of the tenacious and wily conservative minority.)

⌘ October 13, 1964: The debate begins on **the document dealing with priestly life and ministry**. The document, which had been distributed the year before, has now been reduced to a series of propositions. This is seen as insufficient by most in the council. Cardinal Meyer of Chicago speaks for many when he points out that the council has fully debated the place of bishops and the place of the laity in the modern Church. There should also be, he says, a full debate on the place of priests lest the outcome be a medieval priesthood in an otherwise modern world. On October 19, an overwhelming majority sends the document back to its commission for revision.

⌘ October 15, 1964: **The document on Eastern Churches** is introduced for debate. In general, the schema is seen as insufficient in dealing with the place of the patriarchs and is thought by many to Romanize the East. Eastern Rite prelates are the most vociferous in their criticism.

⌘ October 16, 1964: **A married laywoman** is named America's second female auditor. She is Mrs. Catherine McCarthy, president of the National Council of Catholic Women.

⌘ October 20, 1964: The document dealing with **the Church in the modern world**, known in the council as **Schema 13** and long awaited by all, is introduced for debate. (This document had been called for in the first session by Cardinals Suenens and Montini in their response to the first edition of the schema on the Church.) On the first day of debate, eight cardinals speak on this schema, seven favorably, and the council adopts it as the basis for their debate, something they have not done with many other documents. The debate goes on for a number of days and includes speeches developing the schema's many points.

✠ October 22, 1964: Archbishop John Heenan of Westminster, England, **attacks the schema** on the Church in the modern world as dangerous. It is the work of the *periti*, he says, not the council fathers themselves. His remarks, because of their vehemence, stun the majority.

✠ October 23, 1964: Bishop Guano announces that the pope has reserved to himself the decisions on **birth control** because a commission had been established to study the matter the previous June and the pope does not feel it wise to anticipate the results of that group's work.

✠ October 26, 1964: Bishop Louis Morrow, a Texas-born bishop serving in India, says that he speaks in the name of millions who do not understand the Church's teaching on hell. There is, he says, a **"lack of proportion"** between the sin of eating meat on Friday and the eternal hellfire which is the punishment for such a sin. The current teaching, he goes on to say, puts one who eats meat on Friday in the same category as an atheist or an adulterer.

✠ October 29–30, 1964: The discussion on the section on **marriage and birth control** gets under way. Speakers include Cardinal Dearden (Detroit), who presents marriage as ordered toward God, the love of the couple, and the procreation of children, in that order. Cardinal Leger (Montreal) challenges the status quo by saying that "the intimate union of the spouses also finds a purpose in love." This, he went on to say, is the very purpose of intercourse.

Cardinal Suenens (Belgium) calls for a council commission to work with the papal group studying birth control to insure that the Church's teaching will be in keeping with modern times. "I beg of you, my brother bishops," he says, "let us avoid a new **Galileo affair.** One is enough for the Church."

Patriarch Maximos IV Saigh (Antioch), the eighty-seven-year-old whose words have so often called the council to realism in previous debates, says that this is an "urgent problem because it lies at the root of a great crisis of the Catholic conscience. The faithful," he says, "find themselves forced to live in conflict with the law of the Church, far from the sacraments in constant anguish, unable to find a viable solution between two contradictory imperatives: conscience and normal married life. Frankly," he goes on to say, "can the official positions of the Church in this matter not be reviewed in the light of modern theological, medical, psychological, and sociological science? . . . And are we not entitled to ask if certain positions are not the outcome of outmoded ideas and, perhaps, **a bachelor psychosis** on the part of those unacquainted with this sector of life?" (Boldface type is mine.)

On the other side of the debate, Cardinal Ottaviani says, "I am not pleased with the statement of the text that married couples can determine the number of children they are to have. This has never been heard of before in the Church." Cardinal Browne repeats the scholastic doctrine: "The primary end of marriage," he says, "is **procreation and the education of children.** The secondary end is, on the one hand, the mutual aid of the spouses, and on the other, a remedy for concupiscence [i.e., sexual desire]. (Boldface type is mine.)

Shortly thereafter, the debate abruptly ends. Two days later, Cardinal Alfredo Ottaviani, in a worldwide news conference, says that the Church's teaching on this matter will never change because that teaching is based "on the **natural law and several scriptural texts.**" (Boldface type is mine.)

Before the debate on Schema 13 ends, the council fathers deal with sections on **atheism, the Church and the world, racial discrimination, culture, economic and social life, and nuclear war.**

※ November 6, 1964:   The discussion on Schema 13 (the Church in the modern world) is interrupted so that the **pope can visit the council.** Under pressure from some advisers, he introduces the document on missionary activity and calls for its passage. This document, however, has been poorly drawn together and needs more work. The council's sending the document back to the commission which drafted it is an embarrassment for the pope.

※ November 10, 1964:   The document on **the renewal of religious life** is introduced for debate. The progressives favor a wider view and more thorough renewal of religious life than the first draft provided for, especially where a rigorous monastic regime competes with a heavy workload, causing many religious to leave their communities. Two days later, the council fathers send the document back to its commission for revision.

※ November 12, 1964:   The document on **priestly formation** is introduced for debate. The draft is generally judged acceptable to most, a rare occurrence at the council. The document calls for seminary programs more in keeping with the times, ones that develop the personalities as well as the intellects of seminarians.

❊ November 17, 1964: The document on **Christian education** is introduced for debate. The council fathers find it generally acceptable and add only minor changes.

❊ November 19, 1964: The document on **the Church** is passed, 2,134 to 10.

A discussion on the **sacrament of marriage** is held, and a document calling for a renewal in canon law governing matrimony is sent to the pope for inclusion in a future postconciliar decree.

Cardinal Tisserant, president for the day, announces that no vote will be taken in this session of the council on the document on **religious liberty**. The curialists have taken advantage of a minor rule to manipulate this postponement in order, they hope, to kill the document. Immediately, petitions are circulated on the floor of the council, and nearly 1,000 signers call on the pope to intervene to stop this move. In the end, however, the pope allows the minority to sway him, causing anger, resentment, and hostility. (November 19, 1964, becomes known as **Black Thursday** in council history because of these actions on the part of the conservative party and the pope's failure to counteract them.) The pope does promise, however, that this document will be treated first in the fourth session.

There is also a move on the same day by the same minority to postpone action on the document on **ecumenism.** To please the curialists, the pope sends last-minute changes to this document. Cardinal Bea must write them into the document before the council can vote on it.

There is a general sense in the council that **time is running out** because this was to have been its third and final session. Much work remains to be done, however, on multiple documents, including the important and controversial document on **the Church in the modern world.** The minority has been successful in delaying final action on several items and a sense of gloom is palpable in these final days.

※ November 20, 1964: A large majority approves the declaration on **the Church's relations with non-Christians (*Nostra Aetate*).**

The document on **Eastern Churches** is also approved for promulgation the following day.

Likewise, the document on **ecumenism** is approved, including nineteen out of the forty last-minute changes ordered by the pope.

※ November 21, 1964: **The third session is closed** by Pope Paul VI, who takes the occasion **to proclaim Mary the Mother of the Church,** a move that disappoints the Protestant observers and adds to the generally gloomy feeling at the end of this stormy session.

Three documents are promulgated: The Church, Ecumenism, and Eastern Churches. That there will be a fourth session is also announced. The voting on the documents is as follows:

The Church: 2,151 to 5
Ecumenism: 2,137 to 11
Eastern Churches: 2,110 to 39

THE PERIOD BETWEEN SESSIONS 3 AND 4
November 1964 to September 1965

※ November 28, 1964: Pope Paul VI attends the worldwide **Eucharistic Congress in India,** a trip hailed as successful by most.

- January 1965: The pope orders **a letter sent to the heads of curial offices** in the Vatican reminding them that they have come under heavy criticism, including his own, and that they are to be "docile" as reforms of the Curia itself are announced, presumably soon. There is a growing attitude on the part of the curialists, who are also the minority in the council for the most part, that the bishops of the world cannot be trusted with the scope of the reform they have undertaken at Vatican II thus far. The curialists believe that they alone possess the insight and faith needed to govern the Church, and they fear any further move toward collegiality will diminish their power to do so.

- February 19, 1965: Cardinal Bea visits the **World Council of Churches** international center in Geneva and shares the dais with its president, Pastor Marc Boegner of France, in the Hall of the Reformation. In a historic exchange, both express the hope that cooperation "based on love" will lead to closer unity.

During this interim period, it becomes clear to those working on the commissions that fully reformed, biblically based, uniformly open documents on the matters before the council will not be possible. **Compromise and negotiation will be necessary** if the council is to reach a successful end.

It also becomes clear during this period that the sluggish pace of the first three sessions was due mainly to **the tactics of the curial minority,** demonstrated boldly in their delay of the document on religious liberty.

(This document came to a vote early in the fourth session and passed 1,997 to 224, showing how small the minority really was.) But it is also clear that Pope Paul VI has not acted decisively to counter the minority's tactics. These curial insiders, after all, have daily access to the pope, especially Cardinals Cicognani (secretary of state in the Vatican) and Felici (secretary general of the council). Why does the pope not trust the bishops of the world who have expressed their sentiments so clearly in the council? Why does he bend to the wishes of these insiders, whom he himself wished to reform, rather than the majority of the college of cardinals and bishops?

Vatican observers and the press find Pope Paul worrisome and timid, overly committed to gradualism, unwilling to anger the Curia by acting against its desire for the status quo, and unable or unwilling to make decisions in the face of conflicting advice.

✳ March 7, 1965: Showing his support for the reform of the Liturgy, Pope Paul begins **celebrating Mass in the vernacular** on the very first day it is permitted.

✳ June 10, 1965: Pope Paul VI **"rehabilitates" Galileo Galilei.** (In the early seventeenth century, the Italian astronomer had been humiliated by the Church, which, in 1633, forced him to kneel before the Holy Inquisition and recant his Copernican belief that the sun, not the earth, was the center of the universe. Galileo was then placed under house arrest until his death four years later.)

This rehabilitation by Pope Paul VI does not actually admit error on the part of the Church or the medieval popes involved with Galileo's silencing.

✳ August 4, 1965: During this and other summer general audiences, **the pope speaks of the anxieties** he feels as the fourth session approaches. He speaks of the many issues facing the Church and the "burden they place upon us." Repeatedly, he refers to the fear he has of anything other than very gradual reform. Further evidence of this fear is seen in his failure to enact any meaningful reform in the Curia, despite his repeated calls for such.

- September 12, 1965: The weekend before the opening of the fourth session, Pope Paul issues **his third encyclical, *Mysterium Fidei,*** in which he insinuates that the Catholic faith is threatened by certain nameless quarters where debate and dialogue are taking place. This is seen as a reprimand to the Dutch, Belgian, and French theological circles where a discussion on the nature of the Eucharist is under way.

THE FOURTH SESSION

September to December 1965

- September 14, 1965: **The fourth session of Vatican II opens.** Pope Paul presides at a simple ceremony, lacking the pomp of previous openings. In the homily, he avoids discussion of the issues before the council and calls only for charity in dealing with one another. He also announces his intention to visit the United Nations in the fall. In the best news of all, he announces his intention to establish a synod of bishops to advise him. (The formation of such a group had been called for since the beginning of the council and was part of the movement toward collegiality among bishops.)

- September 15, 1965: **Pope Paul attends the first working meeting** of the fourth session. While there, the *motu proprio* entitled *Apostolica Sollicitudo* is read, actually establishing the synod of bishops promised only the day before. No one had expected such rapid action.

  Also on this day, the document on **religious liberty,** as promised, is reintroduced for discussion. The scope of the document, as made clear by Bishop de Smedt (Bruges, Belgium), is to address the question of "the human and civil right to liberty in religious matters." (That is, the extent to which individuals or groups should be free from coercion in matters of religion.) The document defends the place of conscience in such matters, as well as the notion that doctrine develops over time.

The majority generally favor the revised document, citing the growing worldwide movement toward personal independence and civil liberty, separating civil from religious institutions. The minority caution against separating state and church, citing the Italian experience. One Spanish cardinal (Arriba) says that only the Catholic Church has the right to preach the Gospel. Therefore, he argues, others who want to seek converts in Catholic countries must be suppressed, even by the state. Cardinal Ottaviani declares that only the Catholic Church has a true, natural, and objective right to liberty. The attitude of the minority is in direct contradiction to the spirit of the document on religious liberty.

Those who oppose the document fear it will compromise the claim of the Catholic Church to be the one true Church while others fear basing a person's right to religious freedom on the dignity of the human person. In general, American prelates, coming from their long tradition of religious tolerance in the United States, jubilantly hail the document. (An American, John Courtney Murray, S.J., drafted the document.) Bishops from heavily Catholic countries tend to oppose it, along with the curial minority. Bishops from countries where the Church is undergoing persecution (Communist and Socialist mainly) strongly favor it, including Cardinal Wojtyla of Krakow, who eventually was chosen as Pope John Paul II.

Despite the many speeches in favor, it seems that this declaration is running into trouble and might not come to a general vote in the council at all.

※ September 21, 1965: Pope Paul summons certain council leaders to his apartment in the Vatican and orders that a vote on **religious liberty** be taken at once. (The previous evening, a decision by the council's leadership had decided against taking such a general vote.) Immediately, the secretary general, Archbishop Felici, announces that a vote will be taken. It is. The results are **a landslide for the progressives:** 1,997 in favor, 224 opposed.

With that behind them, the council fathers turn their attention back to the document on **the Church in the modern world (Schema 13).** This unique document, the first ever directed by a council to "all humankind," has been drafted in French because modern thought can be expressed understandably only in a modern language. It is also the only conciliar document made available in other modern languages, rather than in Latin. It is now in its fourth revision and is massive, running eighty pages in length!

The mood of the council as the discussion on Schema 13 gets under way is much more optimistic than at the end of the third session, owing in large part to the establishment of the synod of bishops and the overwhelmingly positive vote on religious liberty.

※ September 27, 1965: The debate on the Church in the modern world sees repeated calls for a strongly worded section condemning **atheism,** especially Marxist atheism.

※ September 29, 1965: The debate on the Church in the modern world turns its attention to **marriage** once again. Many feel the document lacks strength because the pope is reserving to himself the decision about the place of birth control in modern Catholic life, considered by most council fathers as the really big issue of married life today. It is generally felt that the document does not give adequate prominence to the key place of sexual intercourse in the life of married couples.

Father Edward Schillebeeckx gives a well-attended conference on the changing nature of Christian marriage in the modern world.

✳ September 30, 1965:   The long-awaited revised schema on relations with non-Christians, especially the Jews, is released. It quickly becomes known, however, that the curialists who prepared the document omitted **the term** *deicide* even though more than 90 percent of the council fathers had ordered its reinsertion at an earlier meeting of the council. The council fathers want a clear statement that the Jews are not guilty of "God-killing" and never were.

✳ October 1, 1965:   Voting on the declaration on the **pastoral duties of bishops** is concluded and receives overwhelming approval.

The U.S. bishops name a commission to establish formal contact with the **American Jewish community.**

✳ October 4, 1965:   Two events occur simultaneously. First, **the pope travels to the United Nations** in New York City, where he delivers an address, the first ever by a pope, calling on the nations of the world to cease war and disarm themselves. His trip is couched in ecumenical gestures, including a key farewell message from the patriarch of Constantinople, whom the pope had met the previous year in Palestine. Second, the council itself takes up a discussion of that section of the Church in the modern world which deals with **"the community of nations and the building up of peace."**

※ October 5, 1965: **Pope Paul returns** jubilantly from his brief trip to the United Nations and is received by the entire assembly of council fathers. His successful appearance on the world's stage and the more congenial discussion on Schema 13 add to the generally optimistic mood of the council.

Meanwhile, voting is occurring almost daily on various parts of other documents, including the duties of bishops, the life of religious, seminary training, Christian education, and non-Christian religions.

As the debate on the Church in the modern world comes to its end, there is near unanimous agreement that it should outrightly **condemn war** and the keeping of nuclear arms.

※ October 7, 1965: The debate on **missionary activity** is taken up once again.

※ October 11, 1965: The pope announces to the council that he is reserving to himself any change in the Church law about **celibacy for priests.** He sends a letter in which he says he does not wish to infringe in any way on the right of any of the council fathers to express themselves but that he does not deem a public discussion of celibacy to be a good thing and that anyone who wishes to give an opinion should submit it to him in writing. He thus removes this from the council's agenda. His action meets with the general approval of most council fathers.

The document on seminary training passes overwhelmingly in voting this same day.

Archbishop Hallinan of Atlanta calls for a much-expanded role for women in the Church.

❋ October 14–15, 1965: Voting takes place on the document on **non-Christian religions,** which is, in large part, a declaration on the **Jews.** This document has three goals: (1) to stress the close scriptural ties between Christians and Jews, (2) to end the old accusation of deicide often hurled against the entire Jewish people, and (3) to end Christian anti-Semitism. Pope John's idea originally, this document began, in the first session, as a draft solely on the Jews, then was temporarily tagged onto the document on ecumenism in the second session, but it did not meet with the approval of the council fathers on either of these attempts.

Now part of a larger document dealing with Hindus, Buddhists, and Moslems in addition to the Jews, there is still a small minority organized against the document. It passed by a vote of 1,763 to 250.

❋ October 14, 1965: Debate finally begins on the document on **priestly life and ministry,** the final document the council will consider.

❋ October 16, 1965: **Council debate formally ends,** except for certain cases permitted under the rules. This leaves time before the close of the fourth session and the entire council to complete work on already debated texts. A week's recess begins.

❋ October 25, 1965: **The council resumes its business,** dealing with unfinished schemata in preparation for voting on them. Council fathers work informally with their *periti* and each other to complete work, debating and phrasing key passages of the remaining documents, especially the one on religious liberty and the one on the Church in the modern world. Suggestions made during the debates are taken under consideration by the various commissions responsible for preparing the various schemata. This is an opportunity for the council fathers to take up minor points and lobby for their inclusion.

✳ October 28, 1965: Five documents are promulgated by Pope Paul VI. The final voting is as follows:

> **Non-Christian Religions:** 2,221 to 88
> **Pastoral Duties of Bishops:** 2,319 to 2
> **Renewal of the Life of Religious:** 2,321 to 4
> **Priestly Formation:** 2,318 to 3
> **Christian Education:** 2,290 to 35

✳ October 29, 1965: The document on **divine revelation** is sent to the pope for promulgation. (The final negotiations on this document were followed closely by Pope Paul, who sent a letter to the commission doing the work asking them to include Cardinal Bea in the discussions because of his close ties to the other Christian Churches and asking them to reconsider the text with an eye to reaching a wider consensus on three things: the relation of Scripture to tradition, the question of biblical freedom from error, and the historic nature of the Gospels.)

Significantly, in the final wording of the texts of council documents, especially the one on divine revelation, the revisions are largely in the hands of those in the conservative curial minority. Experts among the more progressive majority (and it is a huge majority!) scrutinize the work of this curial minority very closely and often find errors of translation or wording that provide subtle, but significant, changes to the texts that may not be caught by all the council fathers.

The document on religious liberty is still under heavy negotiation. (The notion of religious liberty had first been introduced in 1962 during the first session of the council.)

✳ November 9, 1965 The historic document on **the role of laypeople** in the Church is sent to the pope for promulgation. This is the first document of an ecumenical council to deal with the place of laypeople in the life and ministry of the Church.

A **report on indulgences** is presented by a special commission set up by Pope Paul VI to study the issue. The report is issued as a "nonconciliar" document but is released as a convenience since the council fathers are all in Rome. (The report began as an attempt on the part of the pope to experiment with the new synod of bishops, but the Curia undermined that experiment, and this report was issued instead.)

The report on indulgences is long, and it essentially retains the status quo regarding their nature, offering only minor reforms in the indulgence system. Protestant observers are somewhat shocked to see this since it had been the preaching of indulgences which led Luther to his protest. The reform does, however, reduce the number of plenary indulgences available and does do away with measuring indulgences in days or years. Speaking for many, Father Gregory Baum of Canada says, "Some of us are pained that indulgences should be raised at this moment in what, for lack of a stronger word, can be called an inadequate document."

✳ November 15, 1965: Those council fathers who want the document on the Church in the modern world to outrightly **condemn Communism** make a last, determined attempt to amend the text of the schema to include it.

The petition to include the condemnation is considered by the commission and denied. A note referring to past condemnations is inserted instead.

❈ November 18, 1965:   Two more documents are promulgated today. The votes are as follows:

> **Divine Revelation:** 2,344 to 6
> **Lay Apostolate:** 2,305 to 2.

❈ November 24, 1965:   When the commission completing the revisions in the document on the Church in the modern world turns its attention to **the section on marriage,** the group experiences a **bombshell.** The pope has sent a letter through Archbishop Felici, requiring that certain items be included in this section which would have the effect of solidifying the Church's position relative to **birth control and the dignity of sexual intercourse.** Certain members of the commission are delighted while others are both exasperated and angry. In the following days, the commission, led by Cardinal Dearden of Detroit, Michigan, and on the strength of a clarification from the pope, succeeds in softening the impact of this conservative tactic in a way that meets with the pope's personal approval.

Also during this week, much discussion is held about the section on **war, nuclear war, and conscientious objection to war** in the document on the Church in the modern world. In the end, the right to self-defense is maintained, and a delicate balancing of the interests of various nations regarding military power is sought.

❈ December 4, 1965:   Pope Paul takes part in an **inter-denominational Liturgy of the Word** at the Basilica of St. Paul-Outside-the-Walls, the very church where John

XXIII had earlier announced his intention to call the council. This is the first time since the Reformation, the first time in history, therefore, that a pope prays in this way with Protestants. Paul VI takes his place among them, with very little of the fanfare that normally accompanies papal ceremonies. In his remarks, the pope says, "We would like to have you with us always." More than 1,000 bishops attend, though a small number of others object, but the symbolism of this act is tremendous.

- December 6, 1965: Pope Paul issues a *motu proprio* inaugurating **the reform of the Curia,** long awaited in the council. The name Supreme Congregation of the Holy Office, alarming to many because of its connections with the inquisitions of the past, is changed to Congregation for the Doctrine of the Faith (CDF). The newly organized office will be less concerned, the pope says, with hunting for heretics and more concerned with promoting theological investigation. Finally, those whose teachings and writings are under question will no longer be condemned without being allowed to make their case according to published norms.

  On this same day, the council also approves the document on **the Church in the modern world** with an overwhelming majority and sends it to the pope for promulgation.

- December 7, 1965: A joint declaration from both Pope Paul VI and Orthodox Patriarch Athenagoras I is read simultaneously in Rome and in Istanbul, **lifting the excommunication** they had jointly placed on one another in 1054. In so doing, they also invite the whole world to follow suit and to enter into greater unity. When the representative of the patriarch kneels to kiss the ring of the pope, Paul graciously raises him up and embraces him in a kiss of peace. As the patriarchal representative turns to leave the papal chair, a loud ovation of applause greets him.

Final voting on the remaining documents occurs as well as their promulgation. The results are as follows:

Religious Liberty: 2,308 to 70
Missions: 2,394 to 5
The Church in the Modern World: 2,309 to 75
Priestly Life and Ministry: 2,390 to 4

✖ December 8, 1965: **The fourth session of Vatican II ends and the council is officially closed** at an open-air Mass in front of St. Peter's Basilica.

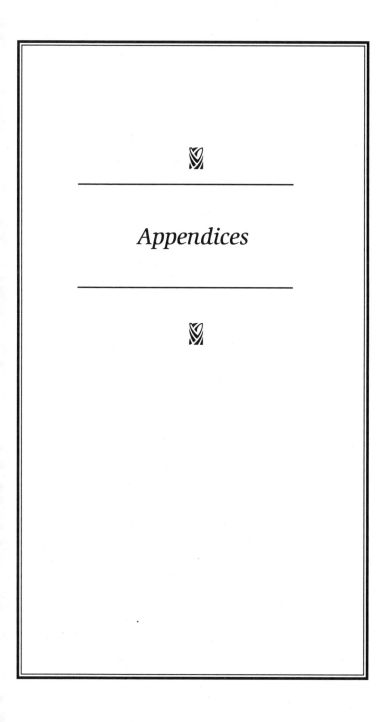

Appendices

Appendix One

※

A Brief Summary of the Documents of Vatican II

PART ONE: THE FOUR CONSTITUTIONS

These major documents set direction for the whole Church.

1. Dogmatic Constitution on the CHURCH

(In Latin, *Lumen Gentium*.)

Approved on November 21, 1964, by a vote of 2,151 to 5.

This strong document was argued by the council from the first day to its passage. It was widely supported in the end and set a major new focus for the Church. It treated several key aspects of the Catholic theology of Church.

(1) The Church, this document says, is a mystery, i.e., "a reality imbued with the hidden presence of God." It is a sacrament: a visible, tangible, audible sign of the invisible, intangible, inaudible divinity. (2) The Church, furthermore, is the whole People of God, including but not identical with its hierarchy alone. (3) Bishops, for their part, are to act collegially, together with the pope, the bishop of Rome. (4) By their very vocation, the laity seek the Reign of God by engaging in "temporal" affairs and ordering them according to the plan of God. (5) The call to holiness is a call to

everyone. (6) The consecrated life of women and men religious is a particular gift to the Church. (7) Christians share the Church with those who have died and who now share life with God in heaven. (8) The memory of Mary is to hold a place of reverence for all.

The document contains 69 articles
in the following eight chapters:

a. The Mystery of the Church
b. On the People of God
c. On the Hierarchical Structure of the Church and in Particular, on the Episcopate
d. The Laity
e. The Universal Call to Holiness in the Church
f. Religious
g. The Eschatological Nature of the Pilgrim Church and Its Union with the Church in Heaven
h. The Blessed Virgin Mary, Mother of God, in the Mystery of Christ and the Church

2. Dogmatic Constitution on DIVINE REVELATION

(In Latin, *Dei Verbum*.)

Approved on November 18, 1965, by a vote of 2,344 to 6.

This strong document states that the Church moves forward in time, developing an ever deeper understanding of what is handed down about the Reign of God and always finding new ways of expressing that.

The document emphasizes that the Word of God is the foundation of divine revelation, and it corrects the understanding that there are two equal sources of revelation, namely, tradition and Scripture. It clarifies that the Word of God is found both in sacred tradition as well as in sacred Scripture. God speaks to us, this document explains, in word and deed and calls forth a response from us. We call this response "faith" and through faith we entrust our whole selves to God. This faith is handed on to all generations by *living* traditions. This faith is contained in one sacred deposit, expressed through the teaching office of the Church whose role and duty it is to serve the Word of God.

The document contains 26 articles in the following six chapters:

a. Revelation Itself
b. Handing On Divine Revelation
c. Sacred Scripture: Its Inspiration and Divine Interpretation
d. The Old Testament
e. The New Testament
f. Sacred Scripture in the Life of the Church

3. Constitution on the SACRED LITURGY

(In Latin, *Sacrosanctum Concilium.*)

Approved on December 4, 1963, by a vote of 2,147 to 4.

This constitution has had the most influence in the emergence of the laity after the council because it updates the Mass, including the role of the laity as ministers in the Liturgy, thus bringing about a sea change in Catholic lay self-identity.

The document seeks (1) to give vigor to the Christian life of the faithful, (2) to adapt what is changeable to the needs of today, (3) to promote union among all who believe in Christ, and (4) to strengthen the Church's mission to all humankind. The constitution declares that the Mass (the Liturgy) is the source and summit of the Christian life.

Therefore, for the Liturgy to be effective, the faithful must (1) be well disposed, (2) know what they are doing, and (3) participate. The document established that some things are changeable (language, books, prayers, music, persons, and places) while some are not (Scripture, bread, wine, prayer over the gifts, eucharistic prayer, communion). It also establishes vernacular in worship. The laity cannot participate in Latin. The document restores the Eucharist as an *act* rather than as a *static devotional object*. This means a downplaying of devotions outside of Mass: rosary, benediction, and so on. The lessening of these devotions is felt very strongly by the average Catholic.

Several "instructions" on implementing the document follow it. The first of these instructions was published before the end of the council.

The document contains 130 articles
in the following eight chapters:

a. General Principles for Restoration and Promotion of the Sacred Liturgy
b. The Most Sacred Mystery of the Eucharist
c. Other Sacraments and the Sacramentals
d. The Divine Office
e. The Liturgical Year
f. Sacred Music
g. Sacred Art and Furnishings
h. Appendix: A Declaration of the Second Vatican Council on the Revision of the Calendar

4. Pastoral Constitution on the CHURCH IN THE MODERN WORLD

(In Latin, *Gaudium et Spes.*)

Approved on December 7, 1965, by a vote of 2,309 to 75.

This important historic document speaks to the Church and to all people about the hopes and dreams of the human family. It is the first document issued by such a council to address the whole world.

"The joy and hope, the grief and anxiety of the people of this age, especially those who are poor or in any way afflicted, this is the joy and hope, the grief and anxiety of the followers of Christ." Modern Christians must look at and trust the signs of the times and understand the world in which they live. (Contrast this with Pius IX's *Syllabus of Errors* in 1864, which says that the pope "cannot and should not be reconciled and come to terms with progress, liberalism, and modern civilization.")

The human person is dignified but many still suffer. Human "conscience is the most secret core and sanctuary of a person where he or she is alone with God." But there is a mysterious aspect to human nature, and conscience is not easily discerned. Modern people live together in a global community of persons for which there must be made available everything necessary for leading a truly human life. Every type of discrimination is to be overcome and eradicated as contrary to God's intent. Science does not conflict with Faith.

The Church lives and acts in the world. "Let there be no false opposition between professional and social activities on the one part, and religious life on the other." It is not "the world against the Church." It is "the world together with the Church."

The document contains 93 articles
in the following nine chapters:

a.   The Dignity of the Human Person
b.   The Community of Humankind
c.   Humans' Activity throughout the World
d.   The Role of the Church in the Modern World
e.   Fostering the Nobility of Marriage and the
     Family
f.   The Proper Development of Culture
g.   Economic and Social Life
h.   The Life of the Political Community
i.   The Fostering of Peace and the Promotion of a
     Community of Nations

PART TWO: THE NINE DECREES

These are significant documents, to be used in further
reflection. They set a pace and direction for further discussion.

1. Decree on the Instruments of
SOCIAL COMMUNICATION

(In Latin, *Inter Mirifica*.)

Approved on December 4, 1963, by a vote of 1,960 to 164.

This relatively weak document is condescending in tone and
is addressed to the media and those who control it. The
document calls for the Church to use modern media to
preach the Gospel. It also calls for the faithful to reject what

is ungodly in the media. The document is seen by most theologians as out of touch with the overall theology of the council. It was one of the first to be passed.

The document contains 24 articles
in the following two chapters:

a. On the Teaching of the Church
b. On the Pastoral Activity of the Church

2. Decree on ECUMENISM

(In Latin, *Unitatis Redintegratio.*)

Approved on November 21, 1964, by a vote of 2,137 to 11.

This document represents a major move forward for the Church. It seeks restoration of ties with other Christians rather than their return to Rome. The document admits that blame for separation exists on both sides and calls for a change of heart to make ecumenism possible. Eucharistic sharing may at times be necessary for the gaining of the grace of unity (n. 8). The document encourages dialogue and calls for the Roman Church to reform itself as part of the process of reunion.

The document contains 24 articles
in the following three chapters:

a. Catholic Principles on Ecumenism
b. The Practice of Ecumenism
c. Churches and Ecclesial Communities Separated from the Roman Apostolic See

3. Decree on the EASTERN CATHOLIC CHURCHES

(In Latin, *Orientalium Ecclesiarum.*)

Approved on November 21, 1964, by a vote of 2,110 to 39.

This minor document gives Rome's perspective on the six main Eastern Rite Churches: Chaldean, Syrian, Maronite, Coptic, Armenian, and Byzantine. It states an ardent desire for reconciliation and clearly proclaims the equality of the Eastern and Western traditions.

The document contains 30 articles
in the following six chapters:

a. The Individual Churches or Rites
b. Preservation of the Spiritual Heritage of the Eastern Churches
c. Eastern Rite Patriarchs
d. The Disciplines of the Sacraments
e. Divine Worship
f. Relations with the Brethren of the Separated Churches

4. Decree on the BISHOPS' PASTORAL OFFICE in the Church

(In Latin, *Christus Dominus.*)

Approved on October 28, 1965, by a vote of 2,319 to 2.

This is a follow-up document to the one on the Church. It gives a job description for bishops and stresses the need for shared decision making (collegiality). The document also calls for bishops to be servant leaders and establishes diocesan pastoral councils.

The document contains 44 articles
in the following four chapters:

a. The Relationship of Bishops to the Universal
    Church
b. Bishops and Their Particular Churches or
    Dioceses
c. Concerning Bishops Cooperating for the
    Common Good of Many Churches
d. General Directive

5. Decree on PRIESTLY FORMATION

(In Latin, *Optatam Totius*.)

Approved on October 28, 1965, by a vote of 2,318 to 3.

This document revises the rules for seminary training which
had been established at the Council of Trent 450 years
earlier. It calls for training in Scripture, pastoral counseling,
ecumenism, history, and personal formation. The document
also allows for local training guidelines to produce priests
more ready to deal with local pastoral realities.

The document contains 22 articles
in the following seven chapters:

a. The Program of Priestly Training to Be
    Undertaken by Each Country
b. The Urgent Fostering of Priestly Vocations
c. The Setting Up of Major Seminaries
d. The Careful Development of the Spiritual
    Training
e. The Revision of Ecclesiastical Studies

f.   The Promotion of Strictly Pastoral Training
g.   Training to Be Achieved after the Course of
     Studies

6. Decree on the APPROPRIATE RENEWAL OF RELIGIOUS LIFE

(In Latin, *Perfectae Caritatis.*)

Approved on October 28, 1965, by a vote of 2,321 to 4.

This document urges religious women and men (1) to return to their roots, that is, their reasons for being founded and (2) to adjust to the needs of changing times in the modern Church. It does not repeat the teaching of Trent that religious life is a superior state to that of the married.

The document contains 25 articles all in one chapter.

7. Decree on the APOSTOLATE OF THE LAITY

(In Latin, *Apostolicam Actuositatem.*)

Approved on November 18, 1965, by a vote of 2,305 to 2.

Although this document has less influence than the constitutions, it is important as the first document in the history of ecumenical councils to address itself to anyone other than the Church's own clergy. The document declares that by virtue of their baptisms, the laity have a ministry, not merely a sharing in the ministry of the ordained. This lengthy document details how the apostolic work of the laity is to proceed and how laypersons are to be prepared for this work.

It also places great emphasis on the importance of each person's role in the establishment of the Reign of God.

The document contains 33 articles
in the following seven chapters:

a. The Vocation of the Laity to the Apostolate
b. Objectives
c. The Various Fields of the Apostolate
d. The Various Forms of the Apostolate
e. External Relationships
f. Formation for the Apostolate
g. Exhortation

8. Decree on the MINISTRY AND LIFE OF PRIESTS

(In Latin, *Presbyterorum Ordinis.*)

Approved on December 7, 1965, by a vote of 2,390 to 4.

This last-minute document does not address the social needs of today's priests. (A later synod in 1970 tried to make up for this weakness.) It calls on priests to support the laity and reaffirms celibacy for priests of the Latin Rite. The document says that, although it is not demanded by the very nature of the priesthood, celibacy seems "suitable."

The document contains 22 articles
in the following four chapters:

a. The Priesthood in the Mission of the Church
b. The Ministry of Priests
c. The Life of Priests
d. Conclusion and Exhortation

9. Decree on the Church's MISSIONARY ACTIVITY

(In Latin, *Ad Gentes.*)

Approved on December 7, 1965, by a vote of 2,394 to 5.

This document encourages retaining local religious customs and incorporating the Gospel into them, a radical idea. It also states that the whole Church is missionary, meaning that all the People of God are called to introduce others to the faith. The document tries to consolidate all the strains of ecclesiology discussed elsewhere.

The document contains 41 articles
in the following six chapters:

a. Doctrinal Principles
b. Mission Work Itself
c. Particular Churches
d. Missionaries
e. Planning Missionary Activity
f. Cooperation

PART THREE: THE THREE DECLARATIONS

These statements of theological position are important for their influence on future dialogue.

1. Declaration on CHRISTIAN EDUCATION

(In Latin, *Gravissimum Educationis.*)

Approved on October 28, 1965, by a vote of 2,290 to 35.

This weak document leaves most of the work to postconciliar development. It is still under study today.

The document contains 12 articles on these topics:

a. The Meaning of the Universal Right to an Education
b. Christian Education
c. The Authors of Education
d. Various Aids to Christian Education
e. The Importance of Schools
f. The Duties and Rights of Parents
g. Moral and Religious Education in All Schools
h. Catholic Schools
i. Different Types of Catholic Schools
j. Catholic Colleges and Universities
k. Coordination to Be Fostered in Scholastic Matters

2. Declaration on the RELATIONSHIP OF THE CHURCH TO NON-CHRISTIANS

(In Latin, *Nostra Aetate*.)

Approved on October 28, 1965, by a vote of 2,221 to 88.

This earthshaking document began as a statement only about the Church's relations with the Jews but was widened to say that the "truth" is present outside the Body of Christ and is to be respected wherever it is found, mentioning in particular Hinduism, Buddhism, and Islam, as well as Judaism. The Catholic Church, it states, encourages dialogue and opens itself to the contributions of these others. Most importantly, the document states that God loves the Jews and that they cannot be blamed as a race for the death of Jesus. The document condemns every form of persecution or discrimination against the Jews.

The document contains five articles all in one chapter.

3. Declaration on RELIGIOUS FREEDOM

(In Latin, *Dignitatis Humanae.*)

Approved on December 7, 1965, by a vote of 2,308 to 70.

This most controversial of council documents began as a chapter in the document on ecumenism. The document allows for the development of doctrine and says that the freedom of persons requires that no one ever be forced to join the Church. The Church claims freedom for itself in this document, but also for all religious practice of every kind everywhere.

The document contains 15 articles all in one chapter.

Appendix Two

※

Interesting Council Lists and Statistics

The ten cardinals named to share the presidency of the council in the pope's absence:

1. Eugene Tisserant, Dean of the College of Cardinals
2. Achille Lienart, Lille, France
3. Ignace Tappouni, Syrian Rite Patriarch of Antioch
4. Norman Gilroy, Sydney, Australia
5. Francis Spellman, New York, USA
6. Enrique Pla y Deniel, Toledo, Spain
7. Joseph Frings, Cologne, Germany
8. Ernesto Ruffini, Palermo, Italy
9. Antonio Caggiano, Buenos Aires, Argentina
10. Bernard Alfrink, Utrecht, The Netherlands

The ten council commissions and their cardinal presidents:

1. Faith and Morals, Alfredo Ottaviani
2. Bishops and Diocesan Governance, Paolo Marella
3. The Oriental Churches, Amleto Cicognani
4. The Discipline of the Sacraments, Benedetto Aloisi Masella
5. Discipline of the Clergy and the Christian People, Pietro Ciriaci
6. Religious, Valerio Valeri
7. The Missions, Gregorio Pietro Agagianian
8. The Sacred Liturgy, Aarcadio Larraona
9. Seminaries, Studies, and Catholic Schools, Giuseppe Pizzardo
10. The Lay Apostolate, the Press, and Entertainment, Fernando Cento

The three other important council leadership posts:

1. Secretariat for Promoting Christian Unity, Augustin Bea, S.J.
2. Technical-Organizational Commission, Gustavo Testa
3. Administrative Secretary, Alberto di Jorio

The twenty-one Orthodox and Protestant groups represented at the council:

1. Russian Orthodox Church (Moscow)
2. Coptic Church (Egypt)
3. Syrian Orthodox Church
4. Orthodox Syrian Church of the East (India)
5. Mar Thoma Syrian Church of Malabar (India)
6. Ethiopian Church
7. Armenian Church
8. Russian Orthodox Church Outside Russia
9. Old Catholic Church
10. Anglican Communion
11. Lutheran World Federation
12. Evangelical (Lutheran) Church of Germany
13. World Presbyterian Alliance
14. Disciples of Christ
15. Friends World Committee (Quaker)
16. International Congregational Council
17. World Methodist Council
18. World Convention of Churches
19. International Association for Liberal Christianity
20. Church of South India
21. World Council of Churches

The six Protestant groups present at the council that did not have official delegates observers:

1. National Baptist Convention

2. Orthodox Theological Institute of St. Serge in Paris
3. St. Bladimir's Orthodox Theological Seminary in New York
4. Free Protestant University in Amsterdam
5. National Council of the Churches of Christ in the USA
6. Protestant religious community of Taize in France

The eligible council fathers in the world at the time the council was called in 1962:

2,908 total

The twelve nations with the largest delegations of bishops and other prelates at the council:

1. Italy, 430
2. USA, 241
3. Brazil, 204
4. France, 159
5. Canada, 97
6. Spain, 95
7. India, 84
8. Germany, 68
9. Argentina, 66
10. Mexico, 65
11. Poland, 64
12. Columbia, 52

The seven major areas of the world and the number of bishops and other prelates that attended from each:

1. Europe, 1089
2. South America, 489
3. North America, 404
4. Asia, 374

5. Africa, 296
6. Central America, 84
7. Oceania, 75

The seven major land areas of the world and the 134 nations who sent delegates:

1. In Africa, 44
2. In Europe, 31
3. In Asia, 23
4. In Central America and the Caribbean, 15
5. In South America, 11
6. In Oceania and Australia, 6
7. In North America, 4

The eight women religious named as council auditors on September 23, 1964:

1. Mother Savine de Valon, superior general of the Religious of the Sacred Heart and president of the Union of Superiors General
2. Mother Mary Luke Tobin, superior general of the Sisters of Loreto in Kentucky, USA, and president of the Conference of Major Religious Superiors of Women's Institutes of America
3. Mother Marie de la Croix Khouzan, superior general of the Egyptian Sisters of the Sacred Heart and president of the Union of Teaching Religious in Egypt
4. Mother Marie Henritee Ghanem, superior general of the Sisters of the Sacred Hearts of Jesus and Mary and president of the Assembly of Major Religious Superiors in Lebanon
5. Sister Mary Juliana of our Lord Jesus Christ, secretary general of the Union of Major Religious Superiors in Germany

6. Mother Guillemin, superior general of the Daughters of Charity
7. Mother Estrada, superior general of the Servants of the Sacred Heart in Spain
8. Mother Baldinucci, superior general of the Institute of the Most Holy Child Mary in Italy

The seven laywomen named as council auditors on September 23, 1964:

1. Dr. Alda Micelli, president general of the Missionaries of the Kingdom of Christ
2. Miss Pilar Belosiool, president of the World Union of Catholic Women's Organizations in Spain
3. Miss Rosemary Goldie, executive secretary of the Permanent Committee for International Congresses of the Lay Apostolate in Australia
4. Miss Marie Louise Monnet, president of the international movement for the apostolate in independent social circles in France
5. Miss Anna Maria Roeloffzen, secretary of the International Federation of Feminine Catholic Youth in the Netherlands
6. Marchioness Amalia Lanzaa, war widow
7. Ms. Idducia Marencoa, war widow

The twelve additional auditors for the fourth session appointed on September 14, 1965:

1. KC Chacko, Catholic principal of a college in India
2. Raoul Delgrange, former president of the International Catholic Children's Bureau in Belgium
3. Frank Duff, founder of the Legion of Mary in Ireland

4. Baron Walter von Loe, chair of the German and International Catholic Farmers' Movements
5. Joseph Fitzgerald, president of Serra International in Miami, Florida, USA
6. Martin Work, president of National Council of Catholic Men in Washington, DC, USA
7. Mother Hermoe Chimy, Sisters of the Servants of Mary
8. Dr. Gertrude Ehrle, German Catholic Women's Union
9. Miss Margarita Mayano Llerena, president of World Federation of Catholic Young Women and Girls in Argentina
10. Miss Gladys Parentelli, vice president, International Catholic Farm Youth Movement in Uruguay
11. Mr. and Mrs. Jose Alvarez Icaza, Christian Family Movement in Mexico
12. Miss Hedwig Skoda, from Czechoslovakia

The eight speakers at Vatican II who spoke in support of a more positive place for women in the Church and who submitted written remarks:

1. Archbishop Paul Hallinan of Atlanta, Georgia, USA
2. Cardinal Leo Suenens of Malines-Brussels, Belgium
3. Cardinal Michael Browne, O.P., of the Roman Curia
4. Bishop Michel Vial of Nevers, France
5. Archbishop Claude Dupuy of Albi, France
6. Bishop Luigi Civardi of the Roman Curia
7. Archbishop Elie Zoghbi of Egypt
8. Coadjutor Bishop Herbert Bednorz of Katowice, Poland

(An additional eight council fathers also made oral speeches demanding a greater role for women in the Church.)

The number of times the council met in session over its four years:

168

The number of public meetings the council held:

10

The number of reports that were read to the council (in Latin):

147

The number of speeches that were made during the course of the four years:

2,212

The number of written comments that the council fathers submitted for amendment:

4,361

The average daily attendance at council meetings:

2,200

The highest attendance at any single meeting:

2,399

The estimated number of ballots cast by the council fathers throughout all the voting in all the meetings over the four years of the council:

1.5 million

The outcome of the voting on the final versions of the various sixteen council documents:

<u>On December 4, 1963</u>
Liturgy: 2,147 yes, 4 no
Communications: 1,960 yes, 164 no

<u>On November 21, 1964</u>
The Church: 2,151 yes, 5 no
Ecumenism: 2,137 yes, 11 no
Eastern Churches: 2,110 yes, 39 no

<u>On October 28, 1965</u>
Non-Christian Religions: 2,221 yes, 88 no
Pastoral Duties of Bishops: 2,319 yes, 2 no
Renewal of the Life of Religious: 2,321 yes, 4 no
Priestly Formation: 2,318 yes, 3 no
Christian Education: 2,290 yes, 35 no

<u>On November 18, 1965</u>
Divine Revelation: 2,344 yes, 6 no
Lay Apostolate: 2,305 yes, 2 no

<u>On December 7, 1965</u>
Religious Liberty: 2,308 yes, 70 no
Missions: 2,394 yes, 5 no
The Church in the Modern World: 2,309 yes, 75 no
Priestly Life and Ministry: 2,390 yes, 4 no

The number of council fathers who died during the course of Vatican II:

242

The number of cardinals who died during the council:

12

The number of officially designated experts in theology, canon law, or other fields who were present during the council:

460

The number of these experts who were diocesan priests:

235

The number of experts who were Jesuits:

45

The number of experts who were Dominicans:

42

The twenty-one Eastern Rites and their estimated number of members in the world:

Alexandrian:

1.	Coptic	170,000
2.	Ethiopian	130,000

Antiochene:

3.	Syrian	185,000
4.	Maronite	2,175,000
5.	Syro-Malankara	300,000

Armenian:

6.	Armenian	140,000

Chaldean:

7.	Chaldean	630,000
8.	Malabar	3,000,000

Byzantine (Constantinopolitan):

9.	Belorussian	30,000
10.	Bulgarian	15,000
11.	Greek	2,300
12.	Hungarian	250,000
13.	Italo-Albanian	62,000
14.	Melkite	1,150,000
15.	Romanian	1,560,000
16.	Ruthenian	460,000
17.	Slovak	400,000
18.	Ukrainian	4,200,000
19.	Krizevci	49,000
20.	Albanian	(unknown)
21.	Russian	(unknown)

The various liturgies of these rites were celebrated during Vatican II on an alternating basis. Most Catholics in the world observe the Western Rite as Roman Catholics.

The five rites of the Eastern Orthodox Church:

Greek Patriarchates
1. Constantinople
2. Alexandria
3. Antioch
4. Jerusalem

Russian Patriarchates
5. Moscow

The Eastern Orthodox Church is not in union with Rome and Rome is not in union with the Eastern Orthodox Church. It was the patriarch of this Church, Athenagoras I, and the bishop of Rome, Pope Paul VI, who met during the council in Palestine and who later mutually lifted the excommunication from one another which had been in place since 1054.

Appendix Three

※

Biographies of Certain Persons Influential Before and During the Council

PART ONE: BEFORE THE COUNCIL

Lambert Beaudin, O.S.B.
Liturgical reformer

A monk of the abbey at Mont-Cesar in Louvain, Belgium, Beaudin is regarded as one of the key figures in the emergence and development of the liturgical movement in the early part of the twentieth century.

As early as 1903, his lectures at a Catholic conference in Malines were used as a basis for much of the liturgical renewal movement. He believed in the education and participation of the laity and sponsored workshops in his abbey aimed at providing people with a deeper love of the rites and texts, which, after the Council of Trent, had taken a second place to rubrics.

Beaudin was a close friend of Virgil Michel of St. John's Abbey in Collegeville, Minnesota, and influenced his launching of a full liturgical movement there. This movement spread across the United States and Canada and influenced the council fathers to proceed with reform at

Vatican II, a reform that was already well under way when the council began.

Beaudin died on January 11, 1996.

Virgil Michel, O.S.B.
Founder of the American Liturgical Movement

A monk of St. John's Abbey in Collegeville, Minnesota, Michel studied in Europe with Lambert Beaudin and others, returning to St. John's in 1925 with a vigorous interest and, more importantly, a plan of action for a liturgical apostolate. His abbot, Alcuin Deutsch, approved, and Michel's short but full career was launched. He taught fervently about the need for the Liturgy to affect Christians interiorly, reducing the exterior rubrics to a more proper place. With an understanding of human nature at the forefront of his approach, Michel taught of the human person's need for the mysterious and communal aspects of Liturgy.

Michel based his life's work on his belief that the Mystical Body of Christ was a fruitful biblical image to communicate the reality of the presence of Christ and of people's relationship to each other. One year after arriving at St. John's with this vision, he established the Liturgical Press and promptly published one of Beaudin's books translated into English, *Liturgy, the Life of the Church*, which had an enormous influence on American liturgical thought. This, along with journals and liturgical institutes, kept Michel in the forefront of the movement until his death in 1938.

He had anticipated the spirit and energy and the vision and reform of Vatican II fully twenty-five years before its time.

Romano Guardini
Parish priest, early liturgical reformer

After experiencing the liturgical celebrations at the Benedictine Abbey of Beuron near Tubingen, Germany, during his college years, Guardini committed himself to liturgical spirituality and the promotion of good preaching in the public worship of the Church. As early as 1915, he began moving the altar away from the wall and seating people on three sides of it, employing liturgical practices in which there was lay participation. His work anticipated much of the reform eventually enacted at Vatican II.

Guardini died on October 1, 1968.

Josef Jungmann, S.J.
Liturgical scholar

Having died in 1956, Josef Jungmann did not see his life's work come to its fruition at the Second Vatican Council, but there is little doubt that much of the reform of the Liturgy there owes its theological development to this tireless scholar who lectured widely in Europe and America. Jungmann was on the faculty at Collegium Canisianum in Innsbruck, Austria. His efforts to research and publish the history and theology of Catholic Liturgy were enormous and his output massive.

Marie-Joseph Lagrange, O.P.
Biblical scholar

Lagrange was an early supporter of a critical approach to biblical scholarship, taking into account textual information which results from archaeological and geographical research. He founded the first Catholic biblical research center in

Jerusalem as early as the 1890s. He also taught about the various kinds of biblical literature, such as law, wisdom literature, poetry, prophecy, liturgical language, and historical accounts.

Lagrange had a prodigious output during his lifetime and, even though out of favor with Roman authorities from time to time, was fully vindicated by Pius XII's *Divino Afflante Spiritu*, which authorized such an approach to Scripture. His work was also the basis of Vatican II's return to a biblical-centered theology. In fact, Lagrange's approach to the Bible is now the dominant one in today's Church.

He died on March 10, 1938.

Prosper Gueranger, O.S.B.
Liturgical reformer

Often cited as the founder of all modern liturgical movements, Gueranger was abbot of the Monastery of Solemes in France. He wanted to restore the Liturgy to its earliest forms, which he considered more pure. Toward this end, he involved the assembly in active participation in chant.

Because of the limited resources available to him, Gueranger's scholarship was not as excellent as later generations would produce. However, his influence spread throughout northern France and the low countries, eventually spilling out of the monastery to affect the place and role of the laity in the Mass.

Gueranger died January 30, 1875.

PART TWO: DURING THE COUNCIL

Cardinal Augustin Bea, S.J.
President of the Secretariat for Promoting Christian Unity

As a Jesuit priest, Cardinal Bea was a biblical scholar who taught Old Testament both in Holland and at the Pontifical Biblical Institute in Rome, where he also served as rector from 1930 to 1949. He was confessor to Pope Pius XII and influenced his encyclical *Divino Afflante Spiritu*, which opened the doors on Catholic biblical scholarship and criticism. He was made a cardinal in 1959 and named to the Secretariat for Promoting Christian Unity shortly thereafter.

At the council, Bea played a significant role as a scholar and statesman, able to bridge differing views because of his own natural tolerance and vision. He influenced the writing of the document on divine revelation, as well as those on ecumenical questions. His overall contribution at the council was immense.

He died in 1968.

Henri de Lubac, S.J.
Historian

A professor of history at the University of Lyons and Fourviere, de Lubac authored almost forty books, some of which eventually brought him into conflict with authorities in Rome for his modern and evolutionary thought. Pope John XXIII, however, named him a consultor to a preparatory commission for Vatican II, and he also served as a *peritus* throughout the council. Because the method employed by the council to establish reform relied so heavily on historical roots, Father de Lubac's voice and research were important.

After the council, however, he became known for his more conservative views.

He died on September 4, 1991.

John L. McKenzie, S.J.
Biblical scholar

A foremost leader in the American Catholic biblical movement which preceded and ran concurrent with Vatican II, McKenzie was influential in part because his work was read so widely by laypeople as well as scholars and in ecumenical as well as Catholic circles. His *Dictionary of the Bible* is considered a basic reference text today.

McKenzie, along with several colleagues, fought conservative forces within American Catholicism for the right to follow the norm laid down by Pius XII's *Divino Afflante Spiritu*, which opened the doors for biblical scholarship based on more than literalism, including historical, editorial, and literary forms of critique. These scholars succeeded in establishing their position and in influencing the documents at the council on divine revelation and religious freedom.

McKenzie died on March 2, 1991.

Yves Congar, O.P.
Theologian

Long before Vatican II convened, its themes of reform were sounded in the writing of Yves Congar, a French Dominican theologian and historian whose focus was a theology of Church. In 1958, he had spoken of the Church as the People of God, not simply its clergy. In *Mystery of the Temple*

(Westminster, Md: Newman Press, 1958, p. 174), Congar wrote, "the people of God, the body of Christ, the Church, really becomes what it is."

In his 1953 book *Lay People in the Church* (Westminster, Md: Newman Press), Congar had called for a much fuller participation of the laity:

"The laity are the Church and make the Church, not by being the subjects of the hierarchical mission which gives structure to the institution, but by having part in the dignity of the Body of Christ" (p. 429).

"The function of the laity, who are set at the junction of the Church and the world, is their own and no one else can fill it; it is necessary to the Church's mission" (p. 431).

The mission of the Church, Congar argued, is not to become larger and more powerful, but to be a faithful minority serving the world. In his imagination, the Church was to be a small community, like the one in which Christ lived.

One of his most controversial books, *Vraie et fausse reforme dans l'Eglise* (Paris: Editions du Cerf, 1950) was never translated into English. It called for the Church to always be in a state of reform, never quitting its self-examination to be certain it faithfully represented the Gospels in each age. Such reform was needed, he argued, for the leadership as well as the structures of the Church.

At the council itself, Congar was involved behind the scenes with many of the schemata, often in the face of controversy and over the objections of the conservative curialists, such as Cardinal Ottaviani. Nonetheless, Congar gained the trust of leading spokespersons for reform.

He died in 1995.

John Courtney Murray, S.J.
Theologian

A giant in American theology, John Courtney Murray was a brilliant and formidable scholar whose views have come to dominate the Church's understanding of religious liberty today. A professor on the pontifical faculty at Woodstock College in Maryland, Murray engaged in a years-long debate in the pages of American theological journals with theologians who believed in traditional Catholic positions regarding separation of church and state as well as questions of ecumenism. Taking his lead from Leo XIII's social and political thought, Murray argued that such separation served both church and state best. His opponents, with the strong support of Cardinal Alfredo Ottaviani of the Holy Office, held to a more traditional view. For them, the union of church and state was the ideal, and any loss of this union was deplorable. They believed that ecumenism was not possible because the Roman Catholic Church was the one true Church and everything else apostate.

Eventually, Murray was required to submit his writings for approval by authorities in Rome, and he withdrew from the fracas. He was also not included as a *peritus* for the first session of Vatican II. Later, at the insistence of Cardinal Spellman, however, he was included and eventually rewrote the declaration on religious liberty, the final version of which bears his stamp.

Murray died in 1967.

Cardinal Alfredo Ottaviani
Pro-Secretary of the Holy Office

Born in Rome in 1890, Ottaviani studied at the Roman Seminary and taught at the Apollinaris and the Urbaniana, both in Rome. In 1926, he moved to a post in the Curia, where he would remain in service for fifty years. Beginning in 1935, he worked in the Holy Office and, in 1953, was named its head. During his tenure there, the Holy Office took various measures against (1) theological, biblical, and liturgical movements such as those that included Congar, de Lubac, and Teilhard de Chardin in France; (2) the ecumenical movement; (3) any sort of rapprochement with Socialists, atheists, or Communists; and (4) any attempt to move away from belief in the ideals of the "Catholic state," such as those advanced by John Courtney Murray in America.

Pope John XXIII did not share Ottaviani's view of the Church and the world, and their differences became public knowledge. Ottaviani's commission prepared texts for the council which were largely designed to conform to the teachings of previous popes and to avoid accommodation to the modern age. But in his opening speech at the council, Pope John spoke of his having grown tired of "prophets of doom" and many thought he was speaking of Ottaviani. Indeed, in the council itself, Ottaviani's work was severely criticized. Rallying a conservative curialist party around him, the cardinal attempted every strategy to prevent what he saw as the dismantling of the Church by the council, but in the end, overwhelming majorities opposed his view.

In 1968, when Pope Paul VI announced a major reform of the Holy Office, including a changed name, Ottaviani offered his resignation, which the pope accepted.

He died on August 3, 1979.

Pierre Benoit, O.P.
Dominican biblical scholar

Prior to the council itself, Father Benoit distinguished himself as a scholar of New Testament Greek and one of the first scholars to draw a distinction between biblical *inspiration* and biblical *inerrancy*. He taught that the Gospels do not provide a portrait of the Jesus of history but rather a portrait of the faith of the early community. He taught that through meditation on faith and selective preservation of the story of Jesus, Christians come to faith themselves. He is probably most well known for his work as New Testament editor on the *Jerusalem Bible*, published before the council in 1956.

His principal contribution at the council came in the last two sessions where he served as an expert, working alongside Cardinal Bea on the document on divine revelation and the one on non-Christian religions. He also contributed to the document on the Church and the one on religious freedom.

Benoit died in 1987.

Karl Rahner, S.J.
Theologian

Karl Rahner was born in 1904 into a Church that was officially fighting against "Modernism" and died in 1984 in a Church that was in the process of thoroughly modernizing itself. Rahner served on the faculty of three universities in Europe: Innsbruck, Munich, and Munster. His published books and articles number more than 2,000, a prodigious output.

Called to the council by both Cardinal Koenig of Vienna and Cardinal Doepfner of Munich, Rahner was one of the most influential theologians at Vatican II.

There has been no more thoroughly systematic a theologian in this century, or perhaps since Thomas Aquinas, than Karl Rahner. He was considered too liberal, however, for the organizers of the council and was not initially invited to sit among the eight hundred bishops and theologians from all over the world who were brought to Rome for preparatory consultation.

Eventually invited, he was not without enemies, however, and in mid-November 1962, Cardinal Ottaviani approached Pope John, asking him to order Rahner to leave Rome. The cardinal feared Rahner's influence at the council would be too far-reaching because he frequently lectured conferences of bishops during their free time in Rome between council meetings.

The pope pointed out that the bishops had invited Rahner to speak and that he himself had received a testimonial signed by three cardinals praising Rahner as an outstanding and faithful theologian. In the end, Rahner remained in Rome for the duration of the council.

Perhaps Rahner's most important contribution to the work of the council was his fundamental notion that grace is offered to humans universally. According to this thinking, to be human is to be graced by God. Grace is, therefore, not restricted to Catholics alone, nor to Christians. It is offered unconditionally by God to all. The articulation of this notion of grace moved many bishops to understand as too narrow the long-held Catholic view that salvation is available only for those within the Church.

In fact, Rahner has been called "the theologian of grace," because of the influence of his work. He restated Catholic theology in such a way that grace came to be understood not only as an utterly free gift of a generous God but also as an intrinsic element, a fundamental aspect, of creation. This could be so, Rahner taught, if it is understood that God freely created nature in the first place to be the embodiment of grace, to be that place where grace is realized. Hence, grace is not something added to nature from outside but intrinsic: coming from nature's deepest, innermost core.

The world, therefore, does not come into contact with grace in the first place through the Church, but rather through contact with its own deepest self. When the Church announces this and accepts this grace, it becomes a visible, audible, tangible sign, or "sacrament" of grace, in the world. The Church does not, however, become the "source" of grace. At the council, this theology of grace opened the door to an appreciation of the truths found in non-Christian religions. Furthermore, grace is present in all human social engagements as well as ecclesial ones. It is, therefore, possible to encounter God in every human situation. Thus, movements that strive for justice, peace, and a free social order become aspects of this.

But most importantly, once it is understood that grace pertains to the here and now, as well as to heaven later, it follows that the Church cannot merely dispense grace like candy from a vending machine, but that members of the Church must take an active role in the Church's life and mission. It flows from this that, to allow for fuller participation, church structures will be more democratic.

For Rahner, God does not break into human history or human experience from outside it, but emerges from within human life, human conscience, and human struggles and glories. God has freely entered into human life in the unconditional gift of Godself, which was presented in the fully human life and death of Jesus Christ. God, therefore, is found in human experience, not in some distant, absent heavenly place.

To those who suggested that believing in God did not belong to the modern age, Rahner answered that in affirming the Christian faith, one affirms the goodness of the world and the meaning of human history. For Rahner, God is found in the most ordinary things of everyday life, for it is there that humans truly experience love, which is where the experience God is found as well.

Karl Rahner died in 1984.

Edward Schillebeeckx, O.P.
Theologian

One of the preconciliar books with the greatest influence, *Christ the Sacrament of the Encounter with God,* was published in 1960 by Schillebeeckx, a Dutch theologian. Widening a Tridentine understanding of sacrament, the book offered a new appreciation for the human condition as wholly other than God's. Since God is utterly Other, utterly supernatural, humans have contact with God only through God's own adaptation to the material world. Hence, Christ is the sacrament of the human encounter with God and God's encounter with humankind. Christ is a sign, or symbol, of the presence of God in the world, and the Church is the sacrament of our encounter with Christ. Therefore, the Church is a sign to the world of God's presence and love for it.

The Church as a whole community assures the world that God is with it through Christ. The seven sacraments of the Church are simply, then, the primary ways through which the Church communicates God's acceptance, forgiveness, radical presence, and powerful love.

Schillebeeckx was present in Rome during the council as one of the advisors there. Like many of the theological advisors, he occasionally lectured on topics within his specialty to update the bishops on recent theological developments. For example, during the fourth session, he gave a well-attended conference on the changing concepts of Christian marriage. This talk influenced the debate toward inclusion of a greater focus on the importance of conjugal love within marriage, rather than the preconciliar focus on procreation.

Hans Küng
Theologian

During the first session of the council, the Holy Office in Rome banned Küng's book *The Council and Reunion*. This book, perhaps more than any other single work, helped form the thinking of the theologians and bishops of the world about the possibility of reform that might occur at the council. His basic position was that reform, including reform of the Roman Catholic Church, precedes reunion of the Christian churches. Küng argued that the separation of the churches was due mainly to the authoritative offices of the Church (first and foremost, the papacy) and not to doctrinal or other practical factors.

In the end, much of the reform Küng called for became reality at the council, although he himself remained outside the graces of the traditionalists.

Godfrey Diekmann, O.S.B.
Theologian

In 1938, Diekmann began to work with Virgil Michel as an associate editor of the magazine *Orate Fratres (Worship)*.

A professor of theology at St. John's, Diekmann was a consultor to the preparatory commission for the council and a *peritus* at the council itself and was appointed to the postconciliar commission that oversaw the implementation of the document on the liturgy.

Bernard Häring, C.S.S.R.
Moral theologian

Häring taught canon law and moral theology at the Redemptorist school of theology in Germany and was closely associated with Romano Guardini at the University of Tübingen. He is well known for his work concerning the renewal of moral theology and was a *peritus* at the council.

Jean Daniélou, S.J.
Patristic scholar

Daniélou's work with students in Paris at the Institut Catholique focused on teaching them how to be both truly and completely Christian and yet at home in the modern times. His scholarship explored the modern movements which seemed to oppose the faith, including the worldviews of Freud, Marx, and atheist writers. He brought this influence to bear on the council itself, especially in its work on the Church's relationship to the world.

After the council, Daniélou felt that the outcomes as they were being implemented were a cause of scandal and a danger to the faith, which caused his critics to consider him a reactionary.

He died in 1974.

Angelo Giuseppe Roncalli
Pope John XXIII

There is often the impression that Pope John XXIII was a simple, peasant priest raised suddenly and without preparation to the papacy. The impression continues that once he was there, he was so naive about church politics and history that he summoned an ecumenical council of the Church, unaware of what its outcomes might be. This idea is terribly wrong. Just as the times called for a council, so also Pope John's entire life prepared him to convene, organize, and host it.

Angelo Roncalli was indeed born a peasant farmer in northern Italy, but he quickly found his way around the entire continent of Europe as well as around the Middle East, especially Turkey. He served in the Italian army and later as a chaplain in World War I. Serving as assistant to his local bishop at Bergamo, he traveled widely, meeting the theologians and bishops who would later have great influence on the Church. The bishop at Bergamo was a warm, wise, and courageous gentleman, a true pastor to his flock. He became Roncalli's teacher and friend.

In 1921, Pope Benedict XV summoned Roncalli to Rome to work in the office that oversaw the finances of the Italian foreign missions. Benedict was a unique pontiff. More progressive and less fearful than others before and after him, he gave Roncalli broad and sweeping authority to restructure the office and to bring together the jealous national mission societies in an attempt to make them more effective. Rising to the task, Roncalli visited all of Europe once again and succeeded in handling devout but proudly nationalistic churchmen.

Four years later he was named archbishop and sent to Sofia where he balanced the delicate relationships between anti-Roman local leadership and the Holy See. In 1934, he was assigned to Istanbul, where he was named apostolic delegate for Turkish and Greek Catholics. He learned the local languages and urged Greek and Turkish pastors to use the vernacular rather than Latin in their liturgical ceremonies.

A liturgical movement, opposed by Roman conservatives, had started as far back as the previous century, influenced by Dom Gueranger's books on the liturgical year. This movement extolled the celebration of the Mass, along with the other sacraments, as essential to deepening the spiritual life of the faithful. It urged active and intelligent participation of the faithful in the rites themselves, something forbidden since the sixteenth century because of its similarity to Protestant worship. Schools had been started at Benedictine abbeys in central Europe to teach Gregorian chant and thereby assist the faithful to take an actual part in the rites of the Mass. The curialists in Rome strongly opposed these so-called "dialogue masses," so it is interesting here and a clue about his own understanding of the Church that Roncalli would encourage such participation on the part of the faithful under his care.

Roncalli remained in Istanbul until after World War II ended and was then appointed papal nuncio to France. There he charmed the entire nation, even the chilly de Gaulle, and polished his abilities to bring together separated factions diplomatically. He learned firsthand how to work amid cultural anticlericalism.

In France, Roncalli also learned about the Church's needs in a "new world" whose political and spiritual lives had to be rebuilt in the wake of a devastating war. He witnessed the experimental "worker priest" movement in France, was aware of the "new theology" brewing in that part of Europe, and personally involved himself in the question of whether the Church there in France, or indeed, in all of modern Europe would continue to decline or would experience a rebirth.

A formative experience for Roncalli in Paris was the rise of UNESCO (United Nations Educational, Scientific, and Cultural Organization). His vision that the Church should be involved and invested in this worldwide educational and cultural movement forced the Holy See to join forces with this rather anticlerical organization. The experience gave the future pope a strong sense of the Church's place in the modern world.

In 1954, Roncalli moved from France to Venice as patriarch. Finally, he told the people of Venice, at age seventy-four, he would be able to enjoy pastoral work which had been his lifelong dream. In Venice, he polished his skills at administration, equipping himself to deal eventually with the many complex administrative problems at the Vatican, especially those associated with the calling of a council.

In October 1958, after Pius XII suffered a fatal stroke, Roncalli was chosen by his brother cardinals as pope. Without hesitation or pause, he brought his charm, skills, and global vision to his work. Amazingly, already by late that same year he wondered aloud to his close confidant and secretary of state, Cardinal Tardini, what he could do to restore the lively faith of the early Church and how to give hope to the modern times. Only a few months after his election, it occurred to him that perhaps the answer would be a council.

John XXIII died on June 3, 1963.

Giovanni Battista Montini
Pope Paul VI

Born in 1898 in northern Italy, Montini was the son of an influential lawyer father and a mother active in local charitable causes. He studied for the priesthood in Rome and entered the papal service shortly after ordination. In 1954, he was sent to Milan as archbishop and eventually made cardinal there. While in Milan, he poured himself into pastoral work.

Although supportive of John XXIII's work to organize Vatican II, he was not outspoken as either a liberal or a conservative. During the conclave in which he was elected, he was chosen on the fifth ballot. He continued the work begun by John XXIII, taking an active and often importantly symbolic hand in the reform of the Church, including key meetings with the archbishop of Canterbury and the patriarch of Constantinople, Athenagoras I. He also visited the United Nations, fought for social justice, reformed the Curia, and eliminated much of the pomp associated with the papacy.

Humanae Vitae, his most famous encyclical, which regulated the use of birth control, was also his most controversial. He seemed to suffer from a degree of indecision at times of crisis during the council but saw himself carefully discerning the needs of the Church during these times.

He died on August 6, 1978.

Appendix Four

⬚

A List of All Previous Worldwide Councils and Their Major Outcomes

1. Nicaea I, 325

By this time, theological debates were well under way in the Church. These debates attempted to define the divinity, especially the relationship among the Father, Son, and Spirit in the Trinity. Schools of thought emerged with various leaders articulating ways of thinking about this.

One such leader was Arius, an Egyptian priest who taught that the Son of God was a "created being" and that there was a time when he did not exist. According to Arius, only the Father was *un*begotten. Hence, the Son was created by the Father, just as humans were. To many other theologians of the time, this seemed to effectively deny the divinity of Jesus Christ. Arius did, however, insist that the Son possessed a dignity which is superior in every way to that which humans possess. He taught his beliefs vigorously.

Followers of Arius created sharp camps and divisions in the Church of the fourth century. On his own authority, the Roman emperor Constantine called the Council of Nicaea to contain Arian thinking and to reunite the Church. Church unity was politically desirable for him.

The council was attended mainly by Greek bishops who could not find a way to effectively argue against Arius until they landed on the Greek term *homoousios*, which means that the Father and the Son are "of one substance."

Many of the statements of faith contained in today's Nicene Creed were formulated or ratified at this council:

"We believe in one God, the Father . . . maker of all things visible and invisible . . . and in one Lord, Jesus Christ, the Son of God, begotten out of the Father, the only begotten . . . generated from the Father, that is, from the being of the Father, God from God, Light from Light, true God from true God. . . ."

The belief in these statements is that Christ comes from the Father's very substance, not by creative actions on the part of the Father. Christ lives within the divine order, "one in being" with the Father. Again, in the Greek tongue in which this council was conducted, the term for that is *homoousios*. At the council, Arius refused to accept this term and was, therefore, condemned. The term stuck.

But *homoousios* is not a term found in Scripture, and using it in a formal definition of doctrine paved the way for formulating theological statements and doctrines with other nonscriptural terms.

2. Constantinople I, 381

Arianism did not go away, nor did the discomfort over the use of nonbiblical terms to describe God. Many bishops had serious reservations about what happened at Nicaea.

The great debate regarding the nature and place of the Son and the Holy Spirit in the divinity continued to rage throughout the fourth century. Another emperor, Theodosius, who ruled the East along with Gratian who ruled the West, called the Council of Constantinople. It reaffirmed the Nicene teaching and added the important notion that the Holy Spirit was also equal to the Father and the Son, forming the Trinity. Constantinople also produced the Nicene Creed (so called because it was mainly formulated at Nicaea earlier in the same century).

Oddly, Pope Damasus I, the bishop of Rome, was neither informed that the council was taking place nor invited to attend. A year later a nonecumenical Roman council accepted all the dogmatic pronouncements of Constantinople, while at the same time rejecting certain pronouncements on church governance and order. This act deepened a political conflict between the East and the West, a division that continues into modern times.

3. Ephesus, 431

At the urging of Nestorius, the patriarch of Constantinople, Theodosius II, the Roman emperor, called the Council of Ephesus to vindicate Nestorius's teachings. He taught that Mary was the mother of Christ (*Christotokos*), but not, thereby, the mother of God (*Theotokos*).

Nestorius had many enemies, and they saw a chance here to embarrass him. They called his position one that could eventually be used to divide the person of Christ into two parts, human and divine.

One such enemy was Cyril, an unscrupulous but brilliant theologian who represented Pope Celestine I in the debates at this council. Cyril's position was accepted by the council as a statement of orthodox faith, namely that the Word truly became flesh through a real "hypostatic" union. In other words, the Word does not simply *reside* in a human but *is* actually human. The Word did indeed become flesh. Therefore, Mary can truly be called the Mother of God (*Theotokos*). Nestorius's views were condemned, and he was deposed as patriarch of Constantinople and exiled to Egypt.

The debates at this council were mainly motivated by political goals and were conducted with a minimum of decorum.

Thus, the council was a bit of a circus and a political disgrace in early church history, but it did affirm that Mary was the Mother of God (*Theotokos*) and led to an agreement two years later which declared that Christ was one person with two natures, one human and one divine. It also prepared the way for the next council, which occurred only twenty years later.

4. Chalcedon, 451

Pulcheria and her soldier husband, Marcian, who ruled the empire following the death of her brother, Theodosius II, called the Council of Chalcedon. Pope Leo I insisted that the bishops follow his views on the nature of Christ, and they agreed that those views, published in his *Tome*, harmonized with the teachings of Nicaea, Constantinople, and Ephesus. Amid wrangling from many schools of thought, the council finally defined the Christian faith by saying that Christians believe in Jesus, who was completely divine and completely human, except for sin.

This council had more than five hundred bishops in attendance, the largest gathering of bishops in the Church to that date. An emotional proceeding, the sessions lasted late into the night under candlelight with cheers, curses, and groans filling the hall during the testimony. Among the bishops, major wrangling occurred over the goings-on of what was called the "robber synod" (which had been held in Ephesus between the councils), where shenanigans succeeded in confusing everything even further. In the end, the papal legates, who presided, succeeded in bringing Pope Leo's *Tome* into full acceptance.

Leo thus won a dogmatic victory at Chalcedon but failed to secure absolute power for the papacy since Constantinople still claimed to share it. Constantinople's claim was expressed in its now famous Canon 28, which granted jurisdiction to itself in certain matters of church governance and internal order. Following Rome's rejection of Canon 28, tensions between Rome (the West) and Constantinople (the East) remained strained and eventually ended in schism.

5. Constantinople II, 553

In the Church of the sixth century, there were those bishops and pastors who followed the teachings of Chalcedon, believing and teaching that Christ as one person did indeed have two natures. But there were also many others who continued to believe that Christ had only *one* nature after his birth, even though he had had two before it. These latter were so successful in spreading their position that Emperor Justinian called the Second Council of Constantinople to reconcile the two positions. Pope Vigilius failed to support him, however, so he had the pope kidnapped and brutalized him into signing the council's decrees. In the end, Justinian's plan failed and the disagreement continued.

This was not a bright moment in church history, however, and the doctrinal scope of this council remains unclear. Its main outcome seems to have been a continuation of the earlier condemnations of Nestorianism.

6. Constantinople III, 680–81

Emperor Constantine IV called the Third Council of Constantinople to patch up his relations with Rome and to strengthen his hand with the Moslems, who were becoming a powerful threat. The council condemned those who believed in yet another understanding of Christ: namely, that Christ had only one will because as the Son of God he could not have contradicted the divine will. This view had been unwittingly approved by Pope Honorius in the 630s.

Constantine's strategy was to consolidate his political position by ingratiating the Church at Rome to himself. This strategy seemed to work for him because this view of the nature of Christ's will was indeed condemned and Honorius was chastised posthumously for supporting it. Along with

Honorius, the council condemned four Eastern bishops, straining East-West relations even further.

7. Nicaea II, 787

A major effort had been under way for sixty years to rid the churches of their icons and all other images because these were thought to lead people into idolatry. The movement, begun by Emperor Leo III, was greatly expanded under his son, Constantine V. They destroyed icons and other images and even tortured and killed those who used them.

The Second Council of Nicaea, called by Empress Irene, who ruled in place of a too-young successor, reversed the movement and legitimated the cult of icons which ended the persecution against those who used them. But the council also specified that adoration was due to God alone, allowing that the use of images could be of assistance to the faithful. More than three hundred bishops attended the council.

8. Constantinople IV, 869–70

The Fourth Council of Constantinople was the last council to be held in the East and the last church council for the next 250 years. It was called to condemn and depose Photius, the patriarch of Constantinople. He later returned to power, but the emperor deposed him again.

9. Lateran I, 1123

The papacy had fallen into serious decline in the tenth and eleventh centuries, having become the plaything of powerful Italian or German families. In the eleventh century, a group of reform-minded popes led a struggle to rid the papacy of vice and corruption. In 1122, Pope Callistus II secured an agreement with the German emperor ending his right to appoint bishops. The pope wanted an ecumenical council to ratify this agreement. Hence, he called a council at the

Lateran palace in Rome, which had been given to the papacy by Constantine in the fourth century. No notes or minutes of this council have survived, but historians know of it from postconciliar documents of various kinds. In attendance were three hundred bishops. The First Lateran Council concluded its work in only twenty-three days.

10. Lateran II, 1139

This three-week council met during the month of April and was attended by five hundred bishops. Pope Innocent II called it to rid himself of an antipope, whose followers were in schism. Innocent enjoyed the support of all major European rulers and, as well, the most powerful church leader of the day, Bernard of Clairvaux, a Cistercian monk. The council fathers voted to force those in schism to abandon their position.

The Second Lateran Council also enforced clerical celibacy for those in orders, beginning with the subdiaconate. (The practice had fallen into decay.) In addition, the council excommunicated a group of heretics.

11. Lateran III, 1179

This two-week council was called to show support for Pope Alexander III in his fight for power against German antipopes appointed by Frederick Barbarossa, the German emperor. The strategy worked.

The Third Lateran Council also set the rules for electing a pope by calling for a two-thirds vote of the cardinals and set requirements for the ordination of bishops. (They must be thirty years old and born in wedlock.) Finally, the council condemned some heretics in France.

This is the first council for which historians have attendance records, showing the names of bishops present from Italy (the largest number), France, Germany, England, Scotland, Ireland, Spain, the Balkans, and Palestine.

12. Lateran IV, 1215

This council was called by the most influential medieval pope, Innocent III. The Fourth Lateran Council ran from November 11 to November 30 of 1215. More than four hundred bishops attended, along with eight hundred abbots and priors and numerous ambassadors from all the kingdoms of Europe.

Following Innocent's genius for canon law, the council dealt with the details of the spiritual life of church members, declaring that all Catholics must receive confession and communion at least annually. It also dealt with the teaching of bishops in their dioceses, passed laws regarding marriage, reformed abuses about relics, and required Jews to wear dis-tinctive markings and stay off the streets during Holy Week.

The Fourth Lateran Council instituted the Inquisition, and Innocent was the first pope to apply force and even torture to end religious opinions not deemed orthodox.

13. Lyons I, 1245

Called in France because holding such a meeting in Italy was not possible due to threats from the German emperor, Frederick II, this council met in three sessions and was a blatantly political event. The bishops present voted to depose the emperor as king of Germany and Holy Roman emperor. Their action had an immediate effect, empowering dissident nobles to elect Frederick's own young son in his place. Unfortunately, other reforms ostensibly on the council's agenda had very little effect, including the reform of the clergy.

14. Lyons II, 1274

Called by Pope Gregory X, this council's achievements are not major. Gregory hoped to reunite the Churches and invited the emperor of Constantinople, the king of Armenia, and the Great Khan of the Mongols to the council. Greek representatives did attend, and a reunion of the two Churches was agreed to but politics sabotaged the meeting and nothing much came of it. What did happen, however, was that a reform of papal elections was again enacted, and the pope convinced the two hundred bishops in attendance to provide him with more money to pay for the Crusades.

15. Vienne, 1311–12

Under pressure from Philip IV the Fair, king of France, Pope Clement V called this council while the papacy resided in Avignon, France. To legitimate his raids on the fortunes of the Knights Templars, the king wanted the pope to condemn the organization. (Philip wanted to use the money to pay for his wars.) The Knights Templars were a religious order founded originally to protect pilgrims during the Crusades. The Knights had, indeed, grown wealthy and powerful, and the pope did not want to condemn them without "consultation." Clement V called the council ostensibly for that consultation, but he invited only select bishops, and the king dominated the sessions through his own agents, using ruthless and terrible torture to secure confessions from the Templars. This scandalous council did little else, tabling once again a move to reform the clergy.

16. Constance, 1414–18

At the time of the Council of Constance, the Church was in the midst of what is known as the Great Western Schism (1378–1417), a mainly internal division between two competing papal households, one in Rome (Urban VI, a tyrant followed by Boniface IX, a clever financier, and then Gregory XII, a pious churchman) and the other in Avignon,

France (Clement VII, a warrior, followed by Benedict XIII, a tenacious politician).

The rulers of Europe divided their allegiance between these two households, raising armies and marching through Europe to attack or defend one another on the basis of their allegiance.

One attempt to heal the schism, a nonecumenical council held in Pisa in 1409, succeeded only in electing a third pope (Alexander V, who died within weeks, followed by John XXIII, a moral and spiritual disaster). The Pisa election was aimed at ending the scandalous schism but only made it worse, with three players now rather than two.

None of the three popes would resign, and few of their loyal followers would move in great numbers to join others, so church scholars and legal theologians decided to try an ecumenical council, held in Constance, a Swiss city, under the patronage of Sigismund of Luxembourg, the Holy Roman emperor, who was committed to the reunion of the Church.

Since the popes were unable to settle the matter of the schism, church scholars argued that the three did not, therefore, have a legal standing. Furthermore, they held that ecumenical councils, not the papacy, hold supreme power in the Church. The scholars put this view into force by electing a pope (Martin V) acceptable to all Catholics and by passing two key pieces of legislation: *Haec Sancta*, which formally declared that ecumenical councils were indeed the supreme authority in the Church, and *Frequens*, which mandated the regular meeting of such councils and established a parliamentary sort of church governance.

This council holds a muddy place in church history. In the first place, it was called initially by the pope elected in Pisa, John XXIII, who really did not have the legal standing to do such a thing. (His name, John XXIII, was, of course, taken later by the pope who called Vatican II.)

John arrived in Constance with fanfare, riding a white horse and clad in the vestments of the Liturgy. A large number of people attended the council at Constance with the hope that it would, finally, bring an end to the schism. Among these were 5 patriarchs, 29 cardinals, 23 archbishops, and more than 500 bishops, along with 300 theologians and canon lawyers and a large number of priests, monks, and laypeople. Bishops voted along with theologians and canon lawyers and even certain laypeople.

The council decided that all three popes would have to resign, which John XXIII agreed to do if the others did as well. He deceived the council, however, and, disguised as a stable worker, escaped the city of Constance and reasserted his authority. When news of this broke, the city of Constance erupted into violence, and a mob pillaged the papal palace in anger. John was eventually hauled back into the council, tried, and deposed.

In Avignon, meanwhile, Pope Benedict XIII also refused to recognize the council's authority, and he, too, was deposed. (A pope in the eighteenth century later took the name Benedict XIII.) So, it would seem, this council was called by Gregory XII (the one from Rome) by default, a fact that makes it possible for modern popes to accept it. Gregory in fact formally convened the council near its actual ending, and then resigned himself, leaving room for the election of Martin V.

Furthermore, no pope in history, including Martin V, has seriously accepted the idea that an ecumenical council has more authority than a pope, and the pronouncements of Vatican II explicitly say that is not so. This leaves the documents of the Council of Constance in an unclear position in the annals of church history.

Who actually elected Martin V? A method of papal election was devised at this radically "democratic" council which provided each of five nations with six delegates who voted along with the cardinals.

Before this council completed its work, it fueled yet another controversy by summoning Jan Hus of Prague, a popular Bohemian theologian with a wide following, to testify on his teachings. The council issued the invitation because Emperor Sigismund wanted Hus's popular movement stopped. Hus expressed great concern for his personal safety, fearing that if he attended this council, his enemies would harm him. But he was assured safe passage. When he arrived at the council, however, he was arrested and forced to undergo a prolonged trial and, finally, the council fathers carried out a sentence of capitol punishment right there before the end of the council: death by burning.

While the Council of Constance did restore unity, it failed to enact badly needed reforms: (1) the papacy was not regenerated by the election of Martin V; (2) the exorbitant demands of rival papal tax collectors continued; (3) the breakdown of church courts remained profound; (4) the absenteeism of bishops remained pronounced; (5) the ignorance and downright immorality of the clergy remained widespread; and (6) the selling of church positions continued everywhere, especially in the Roman Curia, whose excesses were the scandal of Europe.

17. Florence, 1431–45
(also known as Basel-Ferrara Florence-Rome)

Martin V, appearing to accept the decrees of Constance relative to the place of ecumenical councils in church authority, called a council in 1423, in Pavia, only five years after the end of the Council of Constance. The plague forced its move to Sienna, but low attendance forced its closure in the following year, and church historians do not count this as an official council.

Martin called another council at Basel, in Switzerland, but died three weeks after it opened and left a mess for his successor, Pope Eugene IV, to deal with. First, Eugene closed the council because of poor attendance, but the council attendees would not quit their work. They insisted that they, not the pope, had supreme authority in the Church. And many temporal rulers, along with fifteen of the twenty-one cardinals in the Church at that time, supported the attendees.

In the end, Pope Eugene withdrew his decree of closure, and the council took charge of the day-to-day operations of the Church. It made appointments, gave judgments, and took a central management role. The council also stripped the papacy of its ability to raise money by ending its right to tax clergy and to sell indulgences.

When an opportunity presented itself to him, Eugene acted to restore his power. He proposed moving the council to Ferrara in Italy to facilitate a meeting with the Byzantine Church. At Basel, this caused disruption and resulted in fistfights on the council floor as those who agreed with the move fought those who disagreed.

Most of the attendees at Basel might have refused to go to Ferrara had it not been for an ugly scene at Mass that day as both sides read their decrees out loud, simultaneously. Many wept at the terrible confusion. In the end, some participants stayed in Basel and continued operating, but many joined the pope. Eventually those who stayed deposed Eugene and elected their own pope, Felix V.

The Church now had two popes and two councils: a new schism.

Meanwhile, Eugene moved his council once again, from Ferrara to Florence and later on to Rome, where it ended in 1445. The council members who stayed at Basel continued to meet but gradually lost their wind, Felix resigned, and the confusion ended.

18. Lateran V, 1512–17

After the rise and defeat of conciliarism (the idea that councils, not popes, have supreme ruling authority in the Church), popes were reluctant to call any further councils. They feared another conciliar uprising. This meant, however, that no reform of the many abuses present throughout the Church would take place.

There was another reason for the failure to reform the Church, however. It was the absolute corruption of the papacy. Under such popes as Sixtus IV, Innocent VIII, and others, the papacy was guilty of blatant corruption, especially the advancement of the popes' own personal interests and financial gains. These popes freely filled the ranks of the cardinals with their own relatives and unworthy accomplices. Politically powerful, the popes were spiritually bankrupt. No reform would come from these men.

But precisely because the Renaissance popes failed to enact these reforms (which were commonly understood to be necessary), Louis XI of France called a council in Pisa in 1511 (it moved to Milan in 1512), intending to *impose* reform on the Church. Just as the popes feared, Louis resorted to Constance's claim of conciliar supremacy over papal rule. In response, Pope Julius II called the Fifth Lateran Council, which was concluded by his successor, Leo X.

The council's agenda was filled with reform activity. Its leaders wanted to address five things: (1) the ignorance of the clergy, (2) the abuses of the bishops, (3) the temporal activity of the popes, (4) a revision of canon law, and (5) the establishment of more regular councils to continue the reform movement.

But Pope Leo X cared little for the welfare of people's souls and seemed unaware of the breakup of Christianity that was about to unfold before his eyes. The council accomplished nothing.

19. Trent, 1545–63

Pope Paul III was a vigorous, reform-minded pope who acted decisively to end abuses. He appointed reformers, reinstituted the Inquisition, and supported the founding of the Jesuits in 1540.

Eleven years into his papacy, Paul called the Council of Trent and held it in northern Italy, within German imperial territory, to prevent it looking too Italian. Fewer than forty bishops, mainly Italians, attended the first session. (In later sessions, when Calvin got to France and Zwingli to Switzerland, more bishops showed up at Trent.) Despite the poor early turnout, the papal representatives who were present led the council in passing clear doctrinal statements and in basing all reforms on them. In particular, the council was careful to define doctrine on the matter of faith and grace, against the teachings of the reformers.

The Council of Trent, of course, was not a reform council at all. It was the opposite: a reaction to reform. The main task of Trent was to *counter* the reformers of the day: mainly Luther, Zwingli, and Calvin. The council entrenched the Church in practices that these reformers opposed and sought to lock many of the rubrics of the Church into place permanently.

Toward this end, the council established manuals for the training of priests. (The Church used these manuals until Vatican II.) It also (1) warned Catholics against association with Protestants, (2) outlawed Catholic marriages with Protestants, (3) created an index of forbidden books,

(4) articulated official Catholic teaching on faith and grace, and (5) differentiated this teaching from Protestant thought.

The Council of Trent promoted the veneration of the saints, Marian devotions, and devotions to the Eucharist rather than participation in the Liturgy. It rejected the use of vernacular translations of the Bible. For the first time, it set down the number and meaning of the sacraments, confirming traditions that had been in practice since the twelfth century, although not since the apostolic period. The reformers vehemently opposed all these practices.

Most importantly, in its first phase of meetings, the Council of Trent affirmed that the revelation of Jesus Christ is transmitted both through "written Scriptures and unwritten traditions," a position that the reformers utterly rejected.

The council regenerated the papacy, although it rooted its new strength in inflexible tyranny against opponents through the index of forbidden books and the Inquisition. By empowering the Jesuits, under the leadership of Ignatius of Loyola, the Church of Europe developed itself as an institution, building in rapid succession many modern universities and other institutes. Unlike the politicians before him, Ignatius had a genius for communicating the love of God and for developing an interior life based on discernment, not monastic disciplines.

A cornerstone of the entire Tridentine reform movement was the reform of the office of bishop. Successive popes enforced this reform. Under it, bishops were ordered to remain in their own dioceses. Moreover, they were told to spend their time preaching, conducting annual synods, building seminaries, choosing only serious candidates for ordination (those who would agree to live faithfully under the discipline of celibacy), imposing strict discipline on convents and monasteries (which had fallen into decay), and giving good example to all in dress, charity, and modesty. This reform alone reached into every corner of the Catholic world.

The Council of Trent generally affirmed that what was contained in the Catholic Church was "perfect." The council made no attempt to reform doctrine. Instead, it concentrated on the moral life of the members of the Church, arguing that the Church itself was not in need of change and that the eucharistic prayer (known then as the canon of the Mass) was "pure of all error." Further, the council maintained that all the sacraments come directly from the command of Christ and the apostles.

In short, this council was not interested in any church reform as such, but only with a reaffirmation that the Roman Catholic Church teaches faithfully what has always been taught and always would be taught: the purest truth.

In the wake of serious structural reform, a Catholic spirituality began to emerge, including attention to works of mercy and justice; a real zeal for the spread of the Gospel; practices of self-control, such as fasting and abstinence; and private, devotional prayer. More frequent communion was urged, regular confession, and an emphasis on the sacraments as a source of grace. Daily Mass, Benediction of the Blessed Sacrament, and Forty Hours Devotions were all part of this.

Following this reform, new leaders emerged in the late 1500s and early 1600s: Philip Neri, Teresa of Avila and John of the Cross, Francis de Sales and Jane de Chantel. These, among others, led the movement toward greater Catholic piety and personal devotion.

20. Vatican I, 1869–70

Pius IX convened Vatican I in 1869 mainly as a conservative effort within the Church of the nineteenth century. His cardinal advisors suggested an agenda for Vatican I that included many matters which would reassert the control of the Church over the thinking of those times. For example, the cardinals wanted a clear statement of Catholic doctrine on points disputed by the public or by other Christians. They also wanted clear condemnations of what they understood to be theological errors of the day.

The planners of Vatican I also wanted to consider whether the changed conditions of the Church did not call for changes in discipline and whether certain relaxations of ecclesiastical laws would not secure a better observance. There was need, too, they observed, for improvements in the education and instruction of the clergy and for a general raising of the level of clerical life among both diocesan clergy and members of religious orders.

On a note sounding at first blush more like a call for reform, several advisors thought that Vatican I might pave the way for the return to Catholic unity of those separated, either in doctrine or in communion and also for renewed vigor in the Church's missionary activity. Only two of the pope's advising cardinals suggested anything at all about infallibility, a matter that, in the end, dominated the outcome of the council.

Wider consultation around the world about the agenda for Vatican I turned up similar results: the council should deal with and condemn the following principal errors: pantheism, naturalism, rationalism, socialism, Communism, spiritism, and religious indifference. Also the modern Protestant and rationalist teachings in regard to the inspiration of the Scriptures and their authority and interpretation ought to be rejected.

Other suggestions included drawing up a universal catechism and promotion of the Christian life through retreats, spiritual exercises, and sodalities. The reform of canon law was called for. Some prelates wanted to examine the relations of church and state and some even urged open tolerance for liberty of worship and the press and called for a pronouncement that the needs of the Church were compatible with the political needs of the present time.

Vatican I occurred in the age before telephones, FAX machines, copiers, and electric lights. As with earlier councils, no sound systems, translation equipment, nor rapid air travel existed. Council speeches were delivered from a podium, and the council fathers strained to hear. News about world events around them, which played a crucial role in the council itself, came slowly, first as rumors and then through the press. No news wires came into Vatican City in the nineteenth century.

Credentials were clarified carefully for the council. Cardinals, archbishops, bishops, certain abbots, and others from around the world were invited to Rome. A central commission of cardinals decided the final agenda: five subcommissions would deal with the following:

faith and dogma
ecclesiastical discipline and canon law
religious orders
Eastern Churches and foreign missions
politico-ecclesiastical affairs and relations of church
    and state

Select theologians and canonists from around the world were also invited as advisors during the council itself. Fully three-fifths of the bishops who would attend would come from Europe. Even those coming from South America, Africa, and Asia were mainly Europeans assigned to those dioceses. Few native Asians or Africans were present at the council.

One hope for Vatican I was that unity might be restored between the Orthodox Eastern Churches and the Holy See and even that the Protestants might reunite with Catholics.

In September 1868, an apostolic letter was issued "to all Bishops of Churches of the Eastern Rite not in communion with the Apostolic See." The pope's messenger, known as a vicar apostolic, carried the letter to the patriarch of Constantinople. In his letter, Pope Pius first strongly reasserted the primacy of the papacy and then proceeded to invite the patriarch and all others among the Eastern Rite Churches to the council, expressing his strong desire that the schism of West and East would be healed. (By "healing," Pope Pius meant that the patriarchs of the East would all agree once again to give their allegiance to him.)

This effort was thwarted from its inception, however, because the pope's letter got to the press before it got to the patriarch of Constantinople, who returned it unopened via the vicar apostolic who had delivered it. In his reply to the pope, the patriarch said that he had already seen the contents of the letter because he had read it in the press. The patriarch continued by saying that "if his Holiness the Pope of Rome has respect for apostolic equality and brotherhood," he should have sent a letter to each of the patriarchs and synods of the East "as a brother to brethren, equal in honor and degree, to ask them how, where, and in what conditions they would agree to the assembling of a Holy Council." This, the patriarch argued, would have been better than dictating the time and location. He would not, he said, attend. The others in the Eastern Churches followed his cue.

The Anglican bishops were not invited on the grounds that their orders were not valid. The pope's letter of September 1868 to all Protestants and other non-Catholics exhorted Protestants to reconsider their position in the face of the innumerable sects into which Protestantism was broken up and to return to the fullness of the Catholic faith and to allegiance with Rome.

They responded with a statement showing why they could not comply with the exhortation of the pope. Naturally, they also did not attend.

Thus, the hopes for reunion with Rome, held by some of Vatican I's planners, were lost. (By the time of the Second Vatican Council, one hundred years later, a much different approach was taken both to the Eastern Rite Churches as well as to Protestants.)

Despite the foibles in invitations and the naive goals regarding other Christians, Vatican I got under way. During the course of the council's work, which ran from December 1869 to August 1870, leadership emerged, mainly from non-Romans such as Cardinal Manning of England. However, he clearly had a very Roman point of view. The conservatives would dominate Vatican I.

One of the bishops who was present for the opening session on December 8, 1869, wrote of his experience, saying that the council fathers had just returned from the great ceremony of opening the council, which lasted from 8:30 A.M. to 3:30 P.M. It was magnificent, he said, beyond description and well worth a little fatigue. About 660 cardinals, bishops, and abbots were present, and the effect of all those prelates, clad in their official robes, was quite stunning to the observer.

Once assembled and opened, the council got down to work on its prepared agenda as political unrest brewed among the nations of Europe. Political unrest also existed within the council as a movement unfolded to include a strongly worded definition of papal infallibility separated from their statement on the nature of the Church.

At the time of Vatican I, two anti-Roman movements existed within the Church: Gallicanism in France and Josephism in Prussia and central Europe. These movements, which were allied to secular rulers, were mainly reactions to the absolutist and tyrannical behavior of those who worked inside the Vatican and who governed the daily life of the Church.

In opposition to these anti-Roman movements, there emerged equally strong conservative groups, and it was these groups who lobbied at Vatican I for the definition of infallibility. The conservative leaders worked in the background, without an official word being spoken in the council itself. They circulated petitions calling for such a definition. Counterpetitions were likewise circulated, and on March 6, 1870, the pope announced that the matter of infallibility would indeed come before the council for debate.

Led by Cardinal Manning of England, the debate was intense. On May 25, 1870, Manning spoke to the council and appealed to them to act: "The shelving of this question at Trent had disastrous results," he said, "worse would follow should the Vatican Council, after facing it, fail to speak with decisive voice."

A trial vote on infallibility and papal primacy was held on July 13. The majority favored passage and the minority, numbering perhaps 200, was dwindling, as minorities do when standing for evidently losing causes. On July 18, a final vote was taken on the matter and the majority was 533 with only two opposed. Ironically, the voting occurred amidst a great and violent rainstorm with lightening flashing into the aula and thunder rolling overhead. As the final votes came in, a glass window nearly directly above the pontifical throne broke, and its shards fell to the floor.

The vote was announced, applause followed, and the council bishops fled Rome as rapidly as they could. Rumors of war were everywhere. The council had not adjourned, but its members were absent.

The council had passed only one other document, *Dei Filius* (in English, *The Son of God*). This mainly theological document discussed the nature of God, the need for revelation, the nature of faith, and the relationship of faith to reason.

On the very day immediately following the historic vote on infallibility, war was actually declared between France and Prussia. By early August, the French troops serving as the pope's army left Rome to defend France against the warring armies of the Prussians.

The papal states then included a large portion of modern Italy, and with the pope's army out of the way, the Italian nationalist armies wasted no time. By early September, they had invaded the pope's territory and advanced on Rome. On September 20, a siege of Rome began, and after a few hours, local loyalist forces capitulated and Rome was occupied. The pope was a prisoner of the Vatican. One month later the pope issued an apostolic letter suspending Vatican I indefinitely, apparently until more propitious times would allow it to continue.

The council adjourned having taken only one major action: an attempt to strengthen the papacy against the times by its edict on papal infallibility. Many churchmen became triumphalistic in the wake of this new decree; clericalism dominated the Church; and a period of unprecedented legalism descended upon the Church.

No doubt acting in good faith, church leaders saw this declaration of infallibility as a continuation of the laying down of the law in the Church. Only five years before this, Pius IX had issued his *Syllabus of Errors,* which listed modern errors, taking aim at every field of nineteenth-century development: social thought, science, theology, and politics. Defining the doctrine of infallibility as the Italian army stood poised to defeat the papal states in the midst of that thunderstorm in the summer of 1870, with all its epic drama, must have seemed like a final, secure nail in the coffin of progressive thought within the Church.

The council had, however, included many other questions on its original agenda: What is the power of bishops? How does their authority coordinate with that of the pope? How shall the unity of Christians be approached? What is the nature and Catholic definition of religious liberty? These questions and others asked by the preparatory commissions of Vatican I would remain undealt with by a council for a hundred years.

Outside the venue of a council, however, plenty was going on in the Church between Vatican I and Vatican II, mainly due to a movement of theologians and church leaders which was named Modernism.

SUMMARY

Council	Pope	Dates
1. Nicaea I	Sylvester I	May to June 325
2. Constantinople I	Damasus I	May to July 381
3. Ephesus	Celestine I	June to July 431
4. Chalcedon	Leo the Great	October to November 451
5. Constantinople II	Vigilius	May to June 553
6. Constantinople III	Agatho and Leo II	November 680 to September 681
7. Nicaea II	Hadrian I	September to October 787

8. Constantinople IV	Nicholas I and Hadrian II	October 869 to February 870
9. Lateran I	Callistus II	March to April 1123
10. Lateran II	Innocent II	April 1139
11. Lateran III	Alexander III	March 1179
12. Lateran IV	Innocent III	November 1215
13. Lyons I	Innocent IV	June to July 1245
14. Lyons II	Gregory X	May to July 1274
15. Vienne	Clement V	October 1311 to May 1312
16. Constance	Martin V	November 1414 to April 1418
17. Florence	Eugene IV	December 1431 to August 1445
18. Lateran V	Julius II and Leo X	May 1512 to March 1517
19. Trent	Paul III and Pius IV	December 1545 to December 1563
20. Vatican I	Pius IX	December 1869 to July 1870
21. Vatican II	John XXIII and Paul VI	October 1962 to December 1965

Appendix Five

※

A Carefully Annotated Reading List on Vatican II

PART ONE: THE DOCUMENTS

The Documents of Vatican II
Walter M. Abbott, S.J.

Most of the standard writings on the council will use this translation. (Costello Publishing Company, 1975, 1984.)

Vatican Council II
Austin Flannery, O.P.

This is good for postconciliar documents and statements. Also, a second volume shows how the council's decisions are being implemented. (Scholarly Resources, 1975; William B. Eerdmans, New Revised Edition, 1988.)

Decrees of the Ecumenical Councils (two volumes)
ed. Norman P. Tanner, S.J.

This reference book provides English translations of all the documents of each ecumenical council in the entire history of the Church. It has excellent indices. (Sheed & Ward, 1990; Georgetown University Press, 1990.)

Part Two: General Works
on the Council

Destination: Vatican II
Thomas More

This highly interactive and detailed CD-ROM includes all major works on Vatican II including Walter Abbott's edition of the documents, the Daybooks, Xavier Rynne, Bill Huebsch's paraphrase text, timelines, biographies, interviews, and much more! (Thomas More Publishing, 1996.)

The Faithful Revolution: Vatican II
Thomas More

This five part video documentary was derived from more than 170 hours of live interviews with many of the council's participants and observers. It tells the story of Vatican II's legacy in an unbiased and complete fashion. (Thomas More Publishing, 1996.)

The Second Vatican Council and the New Catholicism
G. Berkouwer

Berkouwer was an observer at the council, and he has some interesting observations from a non-Catholic point of view. (William B. Eerdmans, 1965.)

The Theology of Vatican II
Dom Christopher Butler

The excellent introduction to this book gives very helpful background for both Vatican I and Vatican II. The work itself is also excellent, but not for beginners. (Darton, Longman & Todd, 1967; Christian Classics, 1981.)

The Joannine Council
Bernard Häring

Häring was one of the liberal *periti* at Vatican II. He pioneered a whole new approach to moral theology. (Herder and Herder, 1963.)

The Council Reform and Reunion
Hans Küng

This work made Küng a household name. He presents the problems and expectations for the council on the eve of Vatican II. The sale of this book in Rome was banned during the first session of the council. (Sheed & Ward, 1961.)

Vatican Council II
Xavier Rynne

This is a detailed account of the proceedings of the council itself and is still the best for accuracy, style, and astute observation. This version is a condensed edition of Rynne's four volumes, one for each session. (Farrar, Straus and Giroux, 1968.)

A Spirituality of Wholeness: The New Look at Grace
Bill Huebsch

This book offers a treatment of the theology of grace which formed the basis of the work done at the council. It is written in easy-to-read sense lines and common English. (Twenty-Third Publications, 1994.)

Rethinking Sacraments: Holy Moments in Daily Living
Bill Huebsch

Another book by the same author in the same style, this volume details the shift in focus which the council enacted in its reform of the traditional seven sacraments of the Church. (Twenty-Third Publications, 1993.)

American Participation in the Second Vatican Council
Vincent Yzermans

This book is a very complete compilation of speeches and other contributions made by U.S. prelates and *periti* during Vatican II. Its index is outstanding. (Sheed & Ward, 1967.)

Vatican II: An Interfaith Appraisal
Edited by John Miller

Miller edited an excellent group of articles, including many that tell the story of the actual debates at the council. To really gain an insight into how the reforms unfolded, read this. The book is out of print but available in used book stores. (Universary of Notre Dame Press and Association Press, 1966.)

A Man Called John
Alden Hatch

No study of the council is complete without reading a biography of John XXIII. This one is brief, readable, and objective. (Hawthorne Books, 1963.)

A Concise History of the Catholic Church
Thomas Bokenkotter

This classic should be on everyone's bookshelf. There is simply no better, more objective postconciliar history of the Church for readability and indexing. (Doubleday, 1977.)

The Church Emerging from Vatican II
Dennis M. Doyle

This is a very well written and easy-to-read treatment of how the council affected the day-to-day life of the Church. Doyle is a scholar on the council and his book makes wide use of anecdotes and stories as a way of situating the council in today's Church. (Twenty-Third Publications, 1994.)

Council Daybook (three volumes)
Edited by Floyd Anderson

For the most complete story of the council's proceedings from the opening speeches to the closing bell, read this. It can be easily browsed and has a very detailed index if one is looking for something specific. It is only available in used book stores. (National Council Welfare Conference, [1962–63] 1965, [1964] 1965, [1965] 1966.)

Council Speeches of Vatican II
Yves Congar, Hans Küng, and Daniel O'Hanlon

Selected by three leading *periti*, these speeches are also included in the daybooks. But this small volume is more available and easier to hold than they are. (Sheed & Ward, 1964.)

Catholicism
Richard McBrien

It goes without saying that this is a handbook for every Catholic, and it presents the outcomes of Vatican II very faithfully. Everyone should own this book. To make it more affordable, McBrien's book is available in softcover editions. (Winston Press, 1981.)

The Catechism of the Catholic Church

This official, comprehensive treatment of the Catholic faith includes an excellent index which gives generous attention to the impact that Vatican II has had on the modern Church. (Harper San Francisco, 1994.)